THE START OF THE ADVENTURE!

Everyone in camp stood silently staring after the ship which was vanishing toward the horizon, smoke pluming from her funnel. Dolph watched the ship until he could no longer see her even with binoculars. He went back into the house and closed the door. The *Proteus* had been their last link with civilization. Now she was gone. Dolph listened to the voices of the men talking outside. They would be looking to him for leadership and decisions. He could not make any mistakes. Outside, the rising wind wailed down on the camp from the unknown northern wastelands. Perhaps they would be able to uncover the secrets of the Arctic—or perhaps, as so many had before them, they might disappear in the frozen void....

MAN AGAINST THE ELEMENTS: Adolphus W. Greely was originally published by Julian Messner.

Critics' Corner:

"A tremendous story of a versatile pioneer in Signal Corps strategy, military telegraphy, U.S. Weather Bureau record keeping, and relief work during the San Francisco earthquake, as well as extremely heroic leadership. Yet with all this the human qualities as a family man are included. . . . Interesting, action-packed reading."
—*Chicago Schools Journal*

"This is an account of a life which spanned nearly a century, a life of distinguished courage, enterprise, and dedication. . . . Vivid accounts are given of Greely's tragic three-year mission to the Arctic in which all but a few men perished; his agonizing tours in the Philippines, in Puerto Rico, and in Wyoming setting up telegraph lines, and of his work as chief United States signal officer. Written in a clear and readable style, this text should interest 'real' adventure fans." —*Virginia Kirkus Service*

Also recommended by: Library Journal.

About the Author:

IRVING WERSTEIN is one of a rare species—a native-born New Yorker who lives in New York City, his favorite town. He went to P.S. 90 and Richmond Hill High School in Queens and to New York University for two years. While getting started as a magazine story writer Mr. Werstein held a variety of jobs: actor, waiter, camp counselor, factory worker, comedian, reporter. After World War II he embarked on a full-time writing career and sold stories to *The Saturday Evening Post, True, Cavalier,* and many other magazines. His radio and television scripts have been produced in Australia and England as well as the United States, and he has written books for both adults and young people. He is a Civil War buff, likes history, reading, drama, Western movies, long walks, and music.

MAN AGAINST THE ELEMENTS:
Adolphus W. Greely

by Irving Werstein

AN ARCHWAY PAPERBACK
POCKET BOOKS • NEW YORK

MAN AGAINST THE ELEMENTS:
Adolphus W. Greely

Julian Messner edition published 1960

Archway Paperback edition published February, 1968

4th printing.....................September, 1973

Published by
POCKET BOOKS, a division of Simon & Schuster, Inc.,
630 Fifth Avenue, New York, N.Y.

L

Archway Paperback editions are distributed in the U.S. by Simon & Schuster, Inc., 630 Fifth Avenue, New York, N.Y. 10020 and in Canada by Simon & Schuster of Canada, Ltd., Richmond Hill, Ontario, Canada.

Standard Book Number: 671-29600-0.
Library of Congress Catalog Card Number: 60-13264.
This Archway Paperback edition is published by arrangement with Julian Messner. Copyright, ©, 1960, by Irving Werstein. All rights reserved. This book, or portions thereof, may not be reproduced by any means without permission of the original publisher: Julian Messner, a division of Simon & Schuster, Inc., 1 West 39 St.,
New York, N.Y. 10018.
Printed in the U.S.A.

*This Book Is for Paula and Yvie Fraser
Because I Love Them*

Author's Note

IN WRITING THIS DRAMATIZED BIOGRAPHY of General Adolphus Washington Greely, I have developed deep admiration for that dedicated, courageous, and gentle man. His bravery was limitless, his patriotism unbounded. Yet he was no flagwaver, no jingoist. He believed in a strong, but democratic America. During the course of his long life he never committed an act of bigotry. To him every man was equal, regardless of race or religion.

He served with distinction as an officer in a Negro regiment during the Civil War. Among the men he chose for the Lady Franklin Bay Expedition was Sergeant Edward Israel, a Jew.

We live in a troubled time. It is to such unsung heroes as Adolphus Washington Greely that we must look for the strength and courage to persevere, not only as individuals but also as Americans.

No book is ever the work of the author alone. I owe thanks and gratitude to many people: to the staff of the American History Room in the New York Public Library for aiding my research; to the

Author's Note

librarians of the New York Historical Society for similar co-operation; to Miss Candida Donadio of Herb Jaffe Associates for her diplomatic prodding; to my editors, Miss Gertrude Blumenthal and Miss Lee Hoffman, at the Julian Messner Publishing Company, for their patient understanding at missed deadlines; to my six-year-old son, Jack, for displaying a forbearance astonishing in one so young; and to my wife, for everything.

I. W.

New York
May, 1960

Contents

	Author's Note	vii
1.	Prologue	1
2.	War!	7
3.	The Young Soldiers	14
4.	Disaster at Ball's Bluff	26
5.	A Bad Blow	40
6.	The Young Lieutenant	56
7.	Mission on the Border	63
8.	The Weather Bureau	71
9.	A Presidential Bet	78
10.	The Lady Franklin Bay Expedition	86
11.	The Last Outpost	99
12.	The Brink of Eternity	108
13.	The Retreat	115
14.	The Ordeal Begins	122
15.	The Ordeal Ends	130
16.	Through the Years	141
17.	The Curtain Falls	152
	Chronology	163
	Personnel of the Lady Franklin Bay Expedition	167
	Suggestions for Further Reading	169
	Index	171

"To die is easy, very easy—it is only hard to strive, to endure, to live!"

Adolphus Washington Greely to the members of his expedition during the retreat from Lady Franklin Bay to Cape Sabine, August, 1884

• • • CHAPTER I

Prologue

ON MARCH 27, 1935, IN WASHINGTON, D.C., a very old white-bearded man wearing the uniform of a major general, Signal Corps, United States Army, was ushered into the White House. Flanked by high-ranking army officers, he was escorted to the East Room, where President Franklin Delano Roosevelt, governmental dignitaries, and members of the aged general's family were waiting.

Upon entering the room the general saluted the President. Despite his years the old soldier still had an erect military bearing. A tall man, he was broad-shouldered and sturdy. His carefully trimmed beard and steel-framed pince-nez gave him a dignified and scholarly appearance. But there was also a soldierly quality about him. The rows of medals on his tunic were proof of his military talent. He had been decorated by several foreign governments and among his medals were the British Cross of St. George, the French *Legion d'Honneur*, the Russian Order of St. Catherine, and the Italian *Medaglia d'Oro*. He had won many honors—and, on this pleasant March day, he was about to receive from the President of the United States his own country's highest award.

Mr. Roosevelt, leaning on an aide's arm, advanced to him. The President carried a small square leather box. When he stopped in front of the old soldier, press photographers pushed forward with poised cameras.

"General Greely"—the President smiled—"this is truly a special day for you. First, I wish you a happy birthday. Ninety-one is a venerable age."

"Thank you, Mr. President," General Greely said. His voice was clear and strong. Age had embraced him as an old friend and had treated him gently.

"And now, General, I have a pleasant duty to perform," Mr. Roosevelt grinned. He turned to a young army officer standing beside him. "Captain, will you please read the citation?"

The officer stepped smartly forward. He unrolled a parchment sheet and began to read: "For meritorious service and conduct beyond the call of duty, the Congress of the United States of America herewith authorizes the presentation to Major General Adolphus Washington Greely, Signal Corps, Retired, the Congressional Medal of Honor. In the course of his long career, General Greely has displayed devotion and courage which should serve as an example to all Americans."

The old soldier tried to follow the reading, but the captain's words ran one into the other. "For his bravery in the Civil War, 1861–1865 . . . for his

Prologue

pioneer work which helped raise the United States Signal Corps to its present efficiency . . . for his indomitable leadership of the Lady Franklin Bay Arctic Expedition, 1881–1884 . . . for his brilliant work during the Spanish–American War in the Philippine Islands and elsewhere . . . for his organization of relief while assigned as Military Commander of the San Francisco District during the disastrous earthquake and fire in 1906 . . ."

The recital of the general's record continued. Singly, each achievement was enough to have brought him fame. Hearing them recounted this way vividly recalled each exploit to him.

He saw again the desperate Civil War fighting, the Arctic wastelands of Lady Franklin Bay, the dusty prairies, and the Philippine and Porto Rican jungles where he had supervised the stringing of thousands of miles of telegraph wire.

He recalled, too, how he had fought the conservatives within the Signal Corps, the hidebound men who had tried to stop him from introducing the field telephone for military use, who had resisted modernizing the corps. But, despite them, he had succeeded in bringing progress and change.

Now he was ninety-one years old. Ninety-one. During his lifetime the United States had grown. Railroads spanned the country. Automobiles sped along great highways where wagon trains had once rolled. Airplanes flew from coast to coast in hours. He had seen so much happen. So very much.

In 1844, when the general was born, John Tyler was President. During his boyhood James Polk,

Zachary Taylor, Millard Fillmore, Franklin Pierce, and James Buchanan had succeeded to the White House.

Back in 1861, early in the Civil War, as a private in Company D, Nineteenth Massachusetts Volunteers, he had been assigned to guard duty in the corridor outside this very room during a reception given by President and Mrs. Lincoln.

The President—Old Abe himself—had spoken to the awed young soldier. He still remembered Lincoln's words: "Where do you hail from, bub?"

"Newburyport, Massachusetts, sir," he had stammered.

"A Massachusetts man. Good. Thank the Lord for you Bay Staters. What's your regiment?"

"Nineteenth Massachusetts, Mr. President."

"I'll bet you're a pack of wildcats." President Lincoln had smiled, then. He glanced at the closed door. "There'll be fancy goings-on tonight. A real shindig. Oh, I do hate these highfalutin parties. I'd rather be sitting before the parlor fire in my carpet slippers. Well, good luck to you, bub." The lanky man shambled into the reception room and the door closed after him.

The general remembered all the Presidents: Andrew Johnson, Ulysses Grant, Rutherford Hayes, James Garfield, Chester Arthur, Grover Cleveland, Benjamin Harrison, William McKinley, Theodore Roosevelt, William Taft, Woodrow Wilson, Warren Harding, Calvin Coolidge, Herbert Hoover, and now Franklin Roosevelt. Some, the general had served

Prologue

as chief signal officer and known intimately. He had personally met all of them.

What a long time, he thought. Wars, depressions, prosperity, riots, strikes, disasters—yet he had endured and the country had endured. Today he was realizing a dream. The Congressional Medal of Honor. He had waited a lifetime for his recognition. At last it was his.

When the young officer finished reading the citation, President Roosevelt opened the leather box, took out the star-shaped medal that dangled from a blue silken ribbon and slipped the loop over the general's head.

"You richly merit this, General Greely," the President said, shaking his hand.

For the moment the old soldier could only nod his head in acknowledgment. His eyes grew moist. Applause rippled through the room. Even the President clapped. The general's daughters, his grandchildren and great-grandchildren clustered about him. Flashpowder flared as the photographers took pictures. Everyone talked at once.

At last someone cried, "That's all for now. The general must rest until his birthday party tonight."

The escort that had led him into the East Room grouped around again. The general turned to President Roosevelt. "Thank you very much, Mr. President."

Roosevelt flashed his grin. "Don't thank me, General. The nation's gratitude is due you—and that medal is its way of showing it."

Another rattle of applause greeted the President's remark. The ceremony was over. The escort led General Greely to a side portico. Sleek limousines were parked in the driveway. An honor guard presented arms. A band played "The Battle Hymn of the Republic." Motorcycle policemen mounted their vehicles.

General Greely lingered on the top step. He gazed out over the White House lawn with its bordering shrubbery and foliage all green in the sunlight. He knew that in the distance, along the Potomac shore, cherry blossoms would soon be blooming. He had already seen some crocuses and daffodils. The springtime had come. This year its arrival saddened him. He loved spring better than any other time of year. But its coming made him regret his age—this was, perhaps, the last spring he would ever know.

The general smiled wistfully; he should feel neither regret nor sadness. After all, in his life, he had been allowed more springs than were given most men.

An officer in his escort touched the general's sleeve. "They're waiting, sir."

The old man inhaled deeply. "Smell the new grass," he said. "The new grass."

He nodded at the anxious young officer. "Don't worry, Lieutenant. I'll not hold up the schedule." He straightened his shoulders and walked down the steps.

• • • CHAPTER 2

War!

THE SUNSHINE WAS BRIGHT AND THE fields were green in the rolling countryside half a dozen miles from Newburyport, Massachusetts, on April 14, 1861. No hint of trouble marred the calm of the flawless spring day.

The farmhouses were white and trim, the acres well tended, the crops (corn, vegetables, rye) plentiful in that fertile region. Apple orchards bore fine fruit both for eating and for pressing into cider. The farmers were prosperous—there were few idlers among the industrious Bay State Yankees.

On one such farm a gangling seventeen-year-old youth was splitting cordwood behind the house. He swung his ax tirelessly. Its rhythmic *thwack*, *thwack* echoed across the freshly tilled fields.

The lanky wood chopper paused at the sound of hoofbeats on the dirt wagon road that led from Newburyport. He lowered his ax and squinted at the oncoming rider. Setting the tool aside, he wiped his hands on his sweat-stained shirt and walked to the wooden fence that ran in front of the farmhouse, watching the approaching rider all the while.

"Howdy, Dave," he said as the horseman came to a rearing halt at the farmhouse gate. "What brings you here?"

The rider slid out of the saddle. He was a husky blond youth, also seventeen years old. "Ain't you heard, Dolph?" he asked.

"Nope. Been busy at chores all day. What's up?" Dolph Greely asked.

His full name was Adolphus Washington Greely; but that was a big mouthful for folks around Newburyport, so everyone simply called him Dolph.

"War! That's what's up!" Dave Garnett cried.

"No! You mean Beauregard really fired on Fort Sumter? You aren't funning me, Dave?"

Dave crossed his heart. "So help me, it's the truth. I came out fast as I could. There's a heap of excitement in town. According to the bulletin they posted at the newspaper office, Bob Anderson surrendered the fort and old Abe Lincoln's calling up seventy-five thousand volunteers," the blond youth said. "It's war!"

"I'm sure glad Lincoln has the gumption to do something. Seventy-five thousand volunteers, huh?" Dolph gripped his friend's arm. His gray eyes danced in excitement. "Dave, by golly, I'm going to enlist!"

"They won't muster you, Dolph! You were only seventeen last month," Dave argued.

"I don't care. The Southerners started it, didn't they? My Pa was an abolitionist—and I'm dead set against slavery and secession, so I have to fight. That's what Pa would want me to do."

"Maybe so, Dolph. But that don't change the fact you're only seventeen. Heck, I'd like to help whip the Rebels—only I'm underage, too. So it seems like old Abe Lincoln's going to have to do without Dave Garnett a while."

"You can talk like that, Dave—but I'm going to join up, no matter what you say," Dolph declared. "I'll figure a way to do it, too!"

Dave Garnett suddenly snapped his fingers. "Hey, Dolph! I have an idea. They're trying to raise a hundred and fifty more men for the Newburyport Rifles—"

"You mean the town militia company? That bunch?" Dolph sneered.

"Wait a minute," Dave cried. "It's the militia that'll be first to go. Maybe, if a fellow showed he was all-fired hot to join, Captain McCall wouldn't be too fussy about regulations. When I left town, the boys weren't exactly breaking their necks to sign up."

"Say, that is an idea, Dave! I'll tell McCall I'm over eighteen—"

"Oh, Dolph, you couldn't keep a straight face. You're no good at lying."

"It won't be a lie when I tell him I'm over eighteen."

"What?"

Dolph crooked a finger at his friend. "Come with me, Dave."

The two boys went to the barn, where a slate

board was nailed to the back of the door. It was used to record the amount of milk the cows produced daily. Dolph took a piece of chalk and wrote the figure "18" on the sole of each shoe.

"Well, won't it be true when I say I'm over eighteen?" he asked, stamping his feet.

"Over eighteen? Over—of course, you're standing over '18'! Here, give me that chalk," Dave cried. He made an "18" on his own soles. "Now we can soldier together."

"I'd best tell Ma what I aim to do," Dolph said, walking out of the barn.

He and Dave were approaching the house when Dolph's mother stepped from the kitchen to the back porch. She smiled at them, wiping her hands on her apron.

"Hello, Dave. I thought that was you riding in from town—" She stopped as they stared gravely at her. "What's the matter? Is something wrong?" she asked.

Dolph rubbed his palms on his denim trousers. "I have something to tell you."

"Now, it can't be that serious, son. There's no need to look so grim."

"Ma, there's war!" Dolph burst out. "They fired on Fort Sumter."

"War is it?" Frances Cobb Greely drew her breath sharply. "War."

She was a small, sweet-faced woman who looked far younger than her forty-five years. No hint of gray touched her black hair. Her figure was trim. Yet there was sadness in her eyes—an expression of grief which had never left her since her husband, John, died five years earlier, in 1856.

She glanced from Dolph to Dave. "This is a terrible day. To think we'll be fighting our own people—"

"President Lincoln wants seventy-five thousand volunteers," Dolph blurted out.

She looked at him anxiously. "You're too young, Dolph. You can't go—"

"My age won't stop me. If they don't take me in Newburyport, I'll run off to Boston. I'll get in."

Mrs. Greely turned to Dave. "You're underage, too, Dave. Are you of the same mind?"

"Yes, ma'am."

Frances Greely shook her head unhappily. "The bugle blows and the young men march off. Boys, even if you do join, you can still be stopped. You're both only seventeen—children, just children!"

"Listen, Ma—the flag, the whole country, everything we believe in is on the block," Dolph said. "I can't wipe out what I've been taught all my life. I can't turn my back now, when there's something to be done about it!" Dolph clenched his fists. "I still hear Pa saying slavery was unchristian. And I remember the night in New Hampshire, on Grandpa Cobb's farm, when he hid the runaways in the hayloft and chased the slave catchers away at the point of his shotgun. The busiest station on the underground railway, he called that barn."

"I know all that, Dolph. Do you really think that'll keep me silent about your age if you enlist?"

"Yes, because you believe as I do."

Frances studied her son. He was six feet tall, lean and broad-shouldered. He had a bony, rugged face and cold gray eyes like his father's. All at once she realized he was a man, not a boy. A man who had the right to make his own decisions. Still she wanted him with her a little longer. It was not easy to give up an only son.

"What's going to happen here? You do a lot of work around the farm," she argued.

"That doesn't cut ice with me, Ma. I'd have gone off to college in the fall, anyway. The farm would have to do without me, then. Besides, Mr. Krebs doesn't really need my help. He can go on running the place just as he's been doing since Pa died. That's no reason."

"But what about college? You have your heart set on engineering."

Dolph chuckled. "If we don't whip the Rebs, this country'll be split so bad there won't be anything for anybody; so I'll be doing what's best for me by helping win the war and get it over fast."

His mother came down from the porch. She reached up and patted his cheek. "You stated your case well, son. I should've expected to hear this from you. After all, your Pa went off to fight in Mexico when you were a baby less than a year old. And Grandpa Cobb was only fifteen when he was a powder boy on Old Ironsides in the 1812 War. If you get past the recruiting officer, I won't interfere."

"Yahoo!" Dolph yelled. He lifted his mother and whirled her around.

War!

"Put me down, you big clown!" she laughed.

Dolph lowered her to the ground and kissed her. "Hang on, Dave. I'll saddle the mare and ride into town with you," he said.

Later Frances Greely stood at the gate looking down the road until the boys disappeared around the bend. She turned back toward the house and whispered, "Dolph, my baby." Then she let the tears come.

CHAPTER 3

The Young Soldiers

AS DOLPH AND DAVE APPROACHED NEWburyport, they heard the bells in town pealing. Mayor Lawrence Townsend had declared this a day of prayer and meditation. All schools and workshops closed. For a while the churches had been crowded, but now a holiday spirit gripped everyone.

With the shipyard, the textile plant, and the iron foundry shut down, idle workers wandered about Main Street, jamming the saloons and grogshops. Flags flew from rooftops and windows. A dozen impromptu parades, some led by a single fifer or a lone drummer, wound through the streets. The Volunteer Firemen's Band formed in the square and tootled patriotic tunes. After a while no one seemed to remember the grave news. Newburyport was having a high time. It was fun to be at large in the April sunshine; to drink whisky, beer, or lemonade and listen to the band.

So far, war was better than a Fourth of July picnic. A fellow could act up for the girls and brag how he was going to enlist and put the muzzle on South Carolina and all the Secesh Rebels.

The Young Soldiers

The two friends rode through the crowds that flooded Main Street, and tethered their horses to the public hitching post near the town hall. The firemen's band was still playing and many people milled about the wide square. Town boys were tussling on the green and Main Street had as much traffic as one might see on a market day.

A large pyramidal tent had been pitched on the grass in the center of the square. Over it hung a crudely lettered cardboard sign: RECRUITING DEPOT—NEWBURYPORT RIFLES.

Dolph pointed to the tent. "Are you still game, Dave?" he asked.

Dave shuffled his feet. "Sure. But I feel kind of funny here." He rubbed his stomach. "All shaky inside."

"Well, how do you expect to feel?" Dolph asked. "I'm all tied up in knots. Let's go, while my legs can still carry me."

They strode to the tent, where militia officers were strutting importantly about. Dolph approached one of them.

"We want to sign up," he said.

The officer eyed him haughtily. "Just stand over there." He pointed. "Over there. The doctor will examine you."

A column of young men stretched raggedly from the entrance of the tent. The boys went to the end of the line and awaited their turn to enter.

"My heart's beating like an old bass drum," Dolph whispered.

"He'll never pass me," Dave moaned. "I feel sick."

But soon they moved inside. A crabby, near-sighted doctor poked and thumped them.

"Fit as a fiddle, you are," the medic growled, peering through his thick glasses. "Go outside. Next!"

Thirty or forty yards from the tent Captain Asa McCall sat at a field table. The recruits ranged in file at the desk. McCall scribbled with a quill pen in a large ledger, looking up now and then to question the man he was enrolling at the moment.

At last Dolph stood before him. "Aren't you the Widow Greely's son?" McCall asked. He was an earnest, balding man about thirty-five years old, a bookkeeper at the Newburyport National Bank.

"Yes, sir," Dolph answered nervously.

McCall stared hard at him. "It seems to me you're not over eighteen, Mr. Greely."

"Yes, sir! I'm over eighteen, right now," Dolph stated. His knees were shaking.

"You'll swear on the Holy Book that you're over eighteen?"

"Oh, yes, sir! I'll swear it!" Dolph said, crossing his fingers.

McCall tugged at his long mustache. "Well—I suppose I must take your word." He scratched away with the pen, pausing to ask Dolph a question every few moments. At last he had finished filling out the form and pushed the enrollment book at Dolph.

"Before you sign, Greely, I want to know if you

understand that you are enrolling in this regiment for a period of three months."

"Yes, sir. I know that."

"Do you understand that this enlistment period may be extended by the governor of this state? And also that this regiment may be mustered into federal service and shipped to any area designated by the President of the United States or the Secretary of War?"

"Yes, sir."

"And are you also aware that by signing this enrollment book you will be placing yourself under military and not civil law?"

"I'm aware of that, sir."

"All right then—sign here." McCall pointed.

Dolph scribbled his name.

The captain beckoned to a fat young man wearing a militia uniform. "Sergeant Brierly, take this man with the other recruits."

"Look alive, you! Follow me!" the sergeant snapped.

"Don't bark at me, Willie Brierly," Dolph protested.

"Address me by my rank, recruit!" Willie roared.

"Sure, if you say so, Willie—but you'd better speak soft to me, or I'll tan your hide proper," Dolph promised, smiling cheerfully.

The waiting recruits snickered and even Captain McCall grinned; for, despite the uniforms and martial airs, the Newburyport Rifles was hardly a military unit. Dolph had known Willie Brierly all his life and the three stripes on Willie's sleeves meant nothing to him—Willie was still Willie.

The unhappy sergeant glowered at Dolph but spoke more politely. After all the volunteers had been enrolled, Captain McCall and his officers trooped into the meeting room of the town hall, where the recruits had been gathered.

"Boys, I know you'll make jim-dandy soldiers," McCall said. "I'm sure you'll bring glory to our town and our great state. We shall march together against the rebel traitors and crush them to the earth!"

He paused dramatically, his hand raised in a wide flourish. The volunteers cheered; Asa McCall was no meek bookkeeper to them—he was the gallant leader they would follow against the enemy.

McCall's hand dropped. He whipped out his sword, the blade glinting in the gaslight. "I pledge our strength, our blood, our very lives!" he cried.

The recruits cheered even louder. McCall's speech was typical of the oratorical style of the day —flowery and emotional. But to these small-town youths and farm boys his words were thrilling, for he made them feel like knights preparing to ride out on a quest.

When all the cheering had died down, the captain sheathed his sword. "Lads, we have completed our mission for today. You are now enrolled in the Newburyport Rifles. But, since we have neither uniforms nor arms for you and will have none until supplied by the state authorities, you may go home. Hold yourself in readiness for the day we take the field. A day that I hope will soon be upon us!"

"All that hurrahing for nothing," Dolph grumbled as the recruits filed from the hall.

"That's a pretty do, all right. Here we're all signed up for soldiers—but I'll be helping Pa in the hay and feed store tomorrow morning just as if nothing happened."

"Well, I'm heading back to the farm," Dolph announced. "See you around, Dave. It was a big day."

"Sure was." Dave chuckled aloud. "Say, wasn't it a caution the way you handled fat old Willie Brierly?"

"Oh, Willie's all right. Just feeling a mite big. I guess that's what wearing a uniform does to a body. We'll be finding out for ourselves pretty darn quick," Dolph said.

After the first excitement over the war, Newburyport settled down to its usual small-town calm. The war might just as well have been taking place on another planet. Life went on for Dolph as placidly as it had before. He helped Mr. Krebs with the farm chores, and one day passed the same as another.

Frances Greely showed neither relief nor satisfaction that her son still remained at home. The war was something she and Dolph rarely discussed. She perhaps felt that by keeping silent about it, the war would disappear like some unpleasant dream.

It did not touch Newburyport for several weeks more. Although the newspapers carried reports of anticipated Southern assaults on Washington, nothing unusual happened in Newburyport. Even when the Sixth Massachusetts, one of the first fully mobilized regiments, had been attacked in the streets of Baltimore by Secessionist mobs and blood was shed, Newburyport remained tranquil.

In New York, Boston, and Philadelphia tremendous Union meetings had been held. Throughout the North the people were rallying. Men joined the army from cities, towns, and villages. Factories and machine shops switched from peacetime production to the manufacture of cannon, rifles, bullets, and other war matériel.

But in Newburyport all stayed peaceful. The boatyard still sent down the ways the trim pleasure craft which had made it famous. No orders had yet come for war vessels. The iron foundry forges roared. Hammers clanged on metal; but the mechanics were fashioning wagon frames, not gun mounts. The looms in the textile plant wove cloth for dresses and draperies—not blue kersey for uniforms.

Yet that spring, even in Newburyport, one smelled war amid the scent of lilac and dogwood. Its signs were on every side. The nation was in upheaval. Newburyport had been granted only a short respite—and so had Dolph.

On May 23, 1861, about five weeks after his enlistment, Dolph received a letter which ordered him to report for a muster of the Newburyport Rifles at 8:00 A.M., May 25, on the town common. The letter directed him to "provide himself with toilet articles, underwear, socks, soap, a towel, and a blanket in good condition."

He arose early on the twenty-fifth—just after daybreak—but not before his mother. Frances was already in the kitchen brewing coffee when Dolph came in. A fine new woolen blanket, neatly rolled, was lying on a chair.

"I put everything in the blanket, son," she said.

"There was no need—I could've done that."

"You wouldn't deny me such a small pleasure, Dolph?" she smiled.

"Of course not, Ma. A new blanket. It cost a lot of money—"

"Oh, hush. Eat your breakfast. I'll make pancakes."

After the meal Dolph took the blanket, kissed his mother good-by, and stepped into the May morning. He had already saddled the mare and hitched her to the gatepost. His mother stood on the porch.

"I'll leave the horse at Dennison's stable. Mr. Krebs can pick her up tomorrow," he called.

"All right, Dolph." His mother smiled to hide her unhappiness. "Take care of yourself, my dear, and write when you can."

"Sure, Ma. I promise." Dolph gulped hard. This parting was far more difficult than he had imagined it would be. "It's time for me to go now." He gave her a peck on the cheek and sauntered away, trying to appear casual. But when he had strapped the blanket to the saddle and was ready to mount the horse, he turned suddenly and ran back to his mother. Putting his arms around her, he whispered, "I love you, Ma."

She clung to him. "Please be careful, Dolph. Don't get hurt or—or—anything—"

He broke away gently. "Don't worry. I can take care of myself. I'll be back, Ma. You'll see—I'll be back real soon." He strode to the mare and swung himself into the saddle. With a cheerful wave of his hand Dolph galloped off.

"God bless you, son," his mother called after him.

The Rifles were formed in three ragged ranks by the time Dolph had stabled the horse and walked to the town common as the church clock struck eight. The firemen's band was out again, playing martial music, and a good-sized crowd was on hand.

The regiment had turned out at full strength: 194 privates, one first sergeant, four buck sergeants, four corporals, one captain, one first lieutenant, and four second lieutenants. After much yelling by the noncoms and officers, the formation was finally completed. Dolph ran across the grass and fell into rank beside Dave Garnett.

After greeting his friend, Dolph asked, "Where's Captain McCall?"

"In the town hall, with Major Crawford," Dave answered.

"Who's Major Crawford?"

Dave grinned impishly. "Nobody. Only the regular army shoulder strap here to swear us into federal service."

The Young Soldiers

"No fooling!" Dolph cried.

"Oh, things are popping. The whisper is that we're shipping out today."

"How can they do that? We don't even have uniforms?" Dolph cried.

"Yes, we do. They came in on the midnight freight from Boston. Bales and bales of uniforms stored in the town-hall basement—rifles, too, cases of them. Dolph, we'll be in the thick of it mighty soon—and, by heck, that suits me fine!"

"Me too," Dolph agreed.

" 'Tenshun! Silence in the ranks! Captain's coming," fat Willie Brierly bawled.

The men gaped and craned toward the town hall. They saw Captain McCall descending the steps with a burly officer in regular army blue.

"At ease," Captain McCall ordered. "This is Major Walter Crawford, Fifth United States Infantry, our mustering officer. When Sergeant Harris calls your name on the roster, please answer. Take over, Sergeant."

First Sergeant Waldo Harris stepped out, saluted the captain, and faced the ranks. He held a sheet of paper in one hand.

"Sing out proper when you hear your name," he snapped.

As the roll call started, Dolph's heart began pounding hard. He was sure everyone could hear it. His throat went dry, but he managed to croak "Here!" when Harris called "Greely, Adolphus Washington, Private."

When the last man had responded, Major Crawford spoke: "Everyone raise his right hand and repeat after me: 'I swear to defend the United States against all enemies domestic and foreign. I further swear to obey the orders of the officers, warrant officers, and noncommisssioned officers placed above me, so help me God!'"

The young voices echoed the oath. "This unit is now mustered into the service of the United States," Crawford announced. "It will hereafter be known as Company D, Nineteenth Massachusetts United States Volunteers. Its period of enlistment is for the duration of the war or three years, whichever is less. Good luck and may God protect each of you."

The recruits and the militiamen shuffled and fidgeted. This was the most important moment of their lives. They were real soldiers now, hired to fight a war for thirteen dollars a month. The way ahead was a strange and frightening one. Only yesterday each man had been following his own path. This was no longer true. From now on they would live the same way and die the same way. A man could remain an individual only within himself.

Later, uniforms and rifles were issued. They took off their civilian clothes and put on the blue suits. Dolph felt uncomfortable in the uniform. The material was stiff and scratchy. His blouse was loose; his trousers were tight. He remembered the old joke about how clothing fit in the army—the quartermaster issued two sizes: too large and too small.

The rifle he held seemed to weigh fifty pounds, not ten. Although he was a good hunter and a crack shot, Dolph wondered if he could actually shoot to kill a man. He also wondered whether he had the courage to face a real battle with flying bullets and screeching shells. Would he stand, or would he run?

I'll find out someday, pretty darn soon, he mused.

Perhaps it might have been some comfort for him to have known that every man in Company D, Nineteenth Massachusetts United States Volunteers, suffered the same doubts and fears about himself.

• • • CHAPTER 4

Disaster at Ball's Bluff

ANY MAN IN COMPANY D, NINETEENTH Massachusetts, who had dreamed of a chance at immediate glory was badly disappointed. The Newburyporters boarded a rattletrap train at their home-town depot and, with the band playing "Auld Lang Syne," headed southward.

The trip seemed endless to Dolph, but at last they reached Washington, after dark, and were marched off to an encampment on the outskirts of the capital.

The camp had been set up in a pasture field. Cows grazed among the tents. The weather turned unseasonably hot and the men were miserable in their heavy woolen uniforms. The other elements of the Nineteenth Massachusetts had already arrived and Company D was forced to accept the worst location for its bivouac area—the boggy bottom land, which proved to be a breeding ground for mosquitoes.

To make things even more unpleasant, the food was bad, the sanitary conditions were unwholesome, and no one seemed to be sure about anything that had to be done.

In a few days Dolph was thoroughly disgusted with the army. "What a life!" he complained to his friend Dave Garnett. "We've done nothing since we came here but dig sump holes that somebody else fills up the next day."

"You know what the boys say?" Dave grinned cheerfully. "There are two ways of doing things—the right way and the army way."

"By gum, I didn't enlist to be a ditch digger!" Dolph cried.

"Of course not," Dave laughed. "You wanted to win eternal fame on the battlefield—and so did I. Well, we're sure a long way from glory."

"We should be learning to march and fight, instead of lollygagging around doing nothing useful that I can see. By thunder! You don't win wars by digging holes and filling them up again!" Dolph exploded. "Nor by saluting fuzzy-chinned shavetails, either!"

"Whoa! Gentle down, Napoleon. Why don't you just mosey over to the War Department and tell old General Scott how you think things ought to be done? He'll appreciate that, I'm sure."

"Maybe I will," Dolph smiled. "Darn you, Dave—a body can't stay mad around you. I never did see such a blamed good-natured person."

There was a flurry of excitement in July. A big battle had started in Manassas, Virginia, near a creek called Bull Run. The Nineteenth Massachusetts was marched toward Manassas at the height of the fighting, on Sunday, July 20, 1861. But the regiment never reached the battle line.

Halfway there, it was halted in a pleasant grove by a fast-running stream and given orders to wait. The regiment smoked, chatted, slept, ate, and went swimming. One could not tell that men were being killed a bit farther south. The Nineteenth Massachusetts could have been out for a summer Sunday picnic. Not a shot was heard and the birds twittered in the trees. The next day the regiment was back in its camp, digging holes, peeling potatoes, and saluting officers.

The summer ebbed away. In early September the outfit broke camp and marched again. This time to Darnestown, Maryland, on the Potomac River, as part of a force under General Charles E. Stone, to guard the river fords against a possible Rebel crossing.

The first night, Company D was sent directly to the water's edge in the most forward position. Captain McCall ordered the soldiers to load their rifles, and the command was passed down the line from man to man. Dolph rammed in a cartridge. Gripping the weapon in his sweaty hands, he peered across the moon-dappled water. Somewhere on the other side the enemy was lurking in the darkness. He was about to "see the elephant," which was soldier slang for going into battle. Now he had good reason for being where he was—to fight a war. But nothing happened that night or at any time.

After a while, life in the field at Darnestown differed very little from camp. True, the company went on patrols along the river and the sentries walked post with loaded rifles—but the war still was far away. The outpost duty was merely routine. The enemy made no move; in fact, no one had even seen a Confederate and the watchword was "All quiet on the Potomac."

But on October 21, 1861, everything changed. Captain McCall came galloping in from a conference with Colonel Geoffrey Fischer, the regimental commander. He leaped from his horse and shouted, "Sergeant Harris, we're moving out in two hours! Full field packs and forty rounds of ammunition for every man."

Dolph tumbled out of his pup tent as the bugle sounded assembly. "Something's up, Dave!" he cried.

"It's about time," was Dave's response.

The ammunition was issued, the packs were rolled, and two hours later the company marched to a wooded area across the Potomac from a steep cliff on the Virginia side called Ball's Bluff. According to rumors this was the beginning of a Union effort to capture Leesburg, Virginia.

By the time the whole regiment was deployed, the fighting had started. Company D was sent to a point about two hundred yards from the water. The thick woods hid the battle area, but the men could see the gunsmoke and hear the shooting. For once, everyone was solemn. No one made jokes. Up ahead was the war. Every few moments cannon boomed.

Dolph cocked an ear to the racket. "Sounds like the Fourth of July, Dave," he said.

"But those aren't firecrackers," Dave was pale, his voice strained. He edged closer to Dolph. "I have a bad feeling I'm not coming out of this."

"Will you shut up and stop acting like a baby?" Dolph grated fiercely. Dave was putting his own feelings into words.

"I can't help it," Dave whimpered.

"I'm as scared as you are! But we've got to be men. We'll do all right—you'll see."

"Maybe. Maybe," Dave whispered. "I'll try, Dolph. I might get killed—but, by heck, I won't run away!"

"Oh, stop it, you won't get killed!" Dolph peered anxiously through the thick foliage. "I sure wish we knew what was going on up there."

Sergeant Harris came running toward them. "On your feet, lads. We're going forward. Stay together and follow me."

They snaked through the woods closer to the river bank. Gunsmoke hung in layers so thick that they could not see the opposite shore. Two flat-bottomed skiffs ferried troops to the Virginia side, where the Confederates were entrenched on the crest of Ball's Bluff. The clumsy skiffs could carry only fifty men apiece and the troops bunched up waiting to embark. The crowding was so bad in places that units became hopelessly entangled. Officers could not find their companies. No one knew what was happening behind the fog of smoke because the troops on the other side had brought no signaling equipment with them.

"We're caught in a stew, all right," Dolph muttered, shaking his head. "No boats, no signals. It's a mess."

At about 4:00 P.M. a sweat-stained runner floundered through the underbrush. "Captain McCall! Captain McCall!" he cried. "Colonel Fischer wants you at the river on the double. The regiment's crossing."

"Men! We're moving out!" McCall shouted.

The white-faced soldiers pushed and shoved toward the water. Dolph felt sweat trickling down his face, although the afternoon had turned chilly. At the water, a skiff loaded to the gunwales with wounded men, lumbered back from Virginia. Some of the injured, dazed and bleeding, sat in numbed silence. Others, torn by fearful wounds, lay groaning.

A few shouted hysterically, "Don't let them send you over! There ain't a chance! Everybody's getting killed!"

McCall drew his revolver. "I'll shoot the first man who repeats that. You're a pack of cowards!"

"You'll find out, Captain!" a voice shrilled. "We've been there and you ain't!"

White-mustached Colonel Fischer spurred his horse to McCall. "Captain, when the wounded are unloaded, put your men aboard. Your company will lead the regiment. Report to Colonel Baker on the other side."

"That's a hot one," a bloody soldier rasped. "Baker's dead!"

"I've had no word about that," Fischer snapped.

"He's dead, all right! I saw him myself!" the soldier argued.

"Never mind. Get the wounded off the boat!" Fischer barked.

The Company D men helped the casualties from the skiff. Those who could walk staggered off to lie down under the trees. The more seriously wounded were carried.

"You ain't coming back, sonny," a grizzled infantryman leered at Dolph. "The Rebs are on Ball's Bluff shooting down—and you ain't coming back."

Dolph fled, afraid that if he stayed even a second longer he would give in to the fear growing within him.

"Be smart and skedaddle while you can, sonny!" the wounded man yelled after him.

For a moment Dolph struggled to keep himself from plunging into the underbrush and hiding. But he ran to the boat where men were scrambling aboard and climbed onto the crowded vessel. He was pressed against Dave, who clutched his rifle, wide-eyed and ashen. The craft was poled into the stream. Bullets splattered in the water all around.

They're shooting at us. They're really shooting at us, Dolph thought.

A man in the prow threw up his arms and pitched overboard. A volley of shots splintered the railing. Dolph stared unbelievingly at the dead men bobbing face down in the slow current. All this seemed to be happening in a wild dream. When the skiff grounded, Captain McCall jumped into knee-deep water and waved his sword.

"Forward, Company D! Forward!" he yelled. A bullet struck him and he pitched forward, lifeless.

The soldiers stood frozen in the boat when McCall fell. A youthful officer wailed, "My God! My God! The captain's killed!"

But First Sergeant Harris vaulted over the gunwale. Snatching up McCall's sword, he charged toward the river bank. "Come on, boys!" he shouted.

Big Sven Petersen, the color bearer, clambered out and planted the flagstaff in the water. "Form on the colors! Show 'em we ain't cowards!" he bellowed.

Somehow Dolph went over the side and waded toward the bank. His fear turned to anger. All he wanted now was to meet those men on the bluff—and so make them pay for killing Captain McCall.

Sergeant Harris kept shouting from the shore and Sven Petersen waved the colors. Everyone surged off the skiff and floundered onto dry land. They clawed to the top of the muddy bank, stumbling on the dead and wounded piled at the river's edge.

The second boatload of Company D men scraped bottom in shallow water. The enemy fire increased and the new arrivals were hit hard. Dolph saw fat Sergeant Brierly kneeling in the water, praying. A second lieutenant flung away his sword and fled. He splashed into deep water and started swimming, but the bullets from Ball's Bluff cut him down.

The confusion grew worse with the entire company ashore. Their lack of training soon told and the men stood helplessly in bunches. Wounded men struggled to board the skiffs which were preparing to recross. The crew of one boat shoved off without waiting to take a full load. The half-empty craft was swiftly poled to the opposite side—but the second skiff, overcrowded, capsized in midstream.

The shrieks of drowning men rose above the guns. No one could aid them and the battle continued. Although the sun was setting and shadows had deepened in the woods, the firing did not slacken. With no officer to take charge, the command of Company D fell on Sergeant Harris.

Flourishing the sword, he cried, "We're doing no good standing here, lads. Move through the woods. That's where the fighting is." He plunged into the underbrush. Petersen followed him waving the colors.

But not a man stirred until Dolph leaped in front of them and pointed his rifle at the woods.

"We came to fight Rebels, didn't we? Well, that's where they are! I'm going with the colors! Who'll join me?" he exclaimed.

With a yell he dashed into the woods. A cry rose from the men. A handful charged after him. Suddenly a reaction flashed through the company. Singly at first, then in bunches, the men poured into the forest, whooping and cheering.

Powder flashes from rifles had set the dry underbrush afire. Wounded men screamed for help amid the flames. Dolph tried not to hear the cries. He knew he could do nothing for them. He ran on, his eyes on the colors.

Company D plowed through the woods in a wild rush. Beyond the trees was a wide clearing that stretched all the way to Ball's Bluff. There a battle line had been formed. Troops stood in rows firing up at the ridge. A mounted officer galloped toward Company D, sword in hand. He was hatless and his uniform was rumpled. The single star of a brigadier general showed his rank. Dolph gasped as he saw it was General Stone himself.

"Line up there! Line up properly!" Stone bellowed. "You're soldiers, not rabble! Who's in command of this mob?"

Sergeant Harris stepped up and saluted. "I guess I am, sir. Our captain's dead, and there ain't any officers left."

Stone shook his head slowly. "Very well, Sergeant. Lead your men to the right of the line. We're about to attack," he said softly. "You're all brave lads!" he called out. Brandishing his sword, he galloped off, gunsmoke swirling around him.

"This way, boys!" Harris cried.

The company fell in at the right flank of the battle line and, for the first time since the dash through the woods, Dolph had a chance to look about. Nearly half of the company appeared to be missing and he could not see Dave. A feeling of dread seized him.

"Dave," he called out. "Dave Garnett! Where are you?"

A soldier beside him tugged at his sleeve. "Save your breath, Greely. I saw your pal get hit back there in the woods."

"Oh, no!" Dolph gasped.

"He wasn't the only one, mate. We lost a lot of good lads," the soldier said.

The next moment General Stone, closely followed by three staff officers, came galloping down the line. The general rose in his stirrups and yanked his horse to a stop.

"Now we're going to give the Rebs a taste of cold steel. Fix bayonets, boys!" he roared.

The command was repeated all down the line. With trembling fingers Dolph drew his bayonet and after some difficulty attached it to the rifle.

"Now, lads, we'll drive 'em, won't we?" the general cried.

"Yes, yes!" the troops roared.

"Then follow me to death or glory! Charge, bayonets! Charge!" Stone spurred his horse and headed for Ball's Bluff. The soldiers surged forward, cheering as they ran, bayonets pointing ahead. Dolph yelled with the others. For a moment there was silence from the Confederate positions. Then a hurricane of lead swept the charging men.

Soldiers fell in bunches and the attack was broken. All at once a part of the line gave. Men dropped their guns and ran. The panic spread— privates and officers both fled. General Stone stared at the rout in disbelief. He rode among the men, beating left and right with the flat of his sword. "Stand fast! Stand fast, you cowards!"

In a few places little groups clustered about regimental and company colors. Sven Petersen waved his flag. "Company D! Company D, rally here!" he bawled.

But only a few answered his call. Dolph was among those who stayed with the colors. The small band from Company D was among the last Union soldiers to quit the field. They backed off slowly, stopping to fire and reload; retreating grudgingly, a step at a time, fighting all the while.

As they retreated through the woods, Dolph kept looking for Dave but did not find him. The underbrush was still burning briskly; the trapped men were still screaming. Dolph thought he heard Dave calling out and dashed toward the fiery brush.

Sergeant Harris yanked him back. "You wouldn't last two minutes in there!" Harris said.

"I'm going to get Dave out!" Dolph struggled to break loose. "I can't let him die like that!"

"Boy, I understand right enough." Harris tightened his grip. "But it won't do any good to throw your life away, too!"

"I won't leave him! I won't!" Dolph shouted wildly.

Harris raised a huge fist. "Are you coming or must I bash you one?"

Dolph stopped struggling. "All right, Sergeant." He glanced back at the fire. "Dave! Oh, Dave!" he whimpered.

"None of that now, Greely!" Harris said. "Many

more good lads'll be gone before this day's bloody work is over." He clapped Dolph on the shoulder. "Now let's get out of here, before the Rebs pick us up by the ears."

They ran along the trail to the river. The gunsmoke was even denser. Breathing was difficult and they could barely see through the thick clouds. On every side, men were running, falling, stumbling to the water. From the woods came a bedlam of shouts, curses, screams, and shots.

At the river, soldiers stripped off their clothing and leaped in. The water was crowded with swimmers splashing to the Maryland side. Someone in authority had remedied the shortage of boats and now scores of small craft plowed back and forth on the river, snatching weary swimmers from the water.

The Southerners did not lessen their murderous volleys, and dozens of men were shot while swimming or sitting in boats. Sergeant Harris gripped Dolph's arm. "Can you swim?" he asked.

Dolph nodded.

"Then let's take to the water," Harris said. "We'll have a better chance than in the boats. At least you can duck under water if you're swimming."

Kicking off their shoes and discarding rifles and packs, Dolph and Harris dived into the Potomac. Although bullets hissed all around, neither was hit —and a little while later they were stretched on the Maryland shore staring back at the smoke-shrouded Virginia side, where the battle was still being fought. Darkness had fallen and they could see the gun flashes against the dusk background.

Disaster at Ball's Bluff

A Union artillery battery had been posted on a rise to try and cover the retreating federal troops. It fired salvo after salvo at the Confederates, and Dolph watched the shells exploding on the crest of Ball's Bluff.

He had had his wish granted—at last he had "seen the elephant"—and now war held no secrets from him. After having lived through Ball's Bluff nothing would ever be quite the same, he thought. Nothing.

• • • CHAPTER 5

A Bad Blow

AFTER THE BATTLE THE BATTERED REGI-ment returned to Darnestown, where new men came to fill the gaps in the ranks. There were still many familiar faces—Sven Petersen stayed as color bearer, Waldo Harris as first sergeant. Dolph even managed to forget Dave—a man could not go on brooding over a single death in war, not even his best friend's.

The regiment went through a rigorous training program. Colonel Fischer drove his men pitilessly. "Next time we fight," he stated, "you will go into battle fully prepared for it—not as you did at Ball's Bluff."

They practiced combat tactics over and over. Right into line. Left into line. Fire by squads. Fire by platoons. Fire by companies. They learned to form a line of battle from a column of twos or fours. To advance as skirmishers and flankers. To attack by squads and companies.

Fischer was tireless and he had, to help him, new officers sent to replace those lost at Ball's Bluff. Thaddeus Taylor, the lieutenant colonel, was a regular who expected every man to work hard and who worked harder, himself, than any one of his men. Major Quintus Markham, another regular, had years of Indian fighting behind him. He taught the regiment to slip silently from tree to tree, to lie motionless behind a hummock.

"In battle old Mother Earth is your best friend and the shovel your most valuable tool," he insisted. "Dig, lads, dig. The enemy can't hurt you if he can't hit you, and nothing stops a bullet better than a mound of dirt."

As a result of his training the Nineteenth Massachusetts was called the "Gopher Regiment." Its men dug rifle pits at every halt in enemy territory. On an overnight bivouac the regimental area was turned into a fortress with trenches and breastworks. It was hard labor—but no Rebel guerilla force could surprise that encampment; no sudden assault could overwhelm a position held by the Nineteenth.

In January, 1862, Dolph was promoted to corporal. He was the youngest two-striper in the regiment, not yet eighteen. Some of his tentmates boasted he was the youngest in the Army of the Potomac—which may well have been so.

The Army of the Potomac, under the command of General George Brinton McClellan, was molded into a fighting force. The men were ready for combat. Mountains of ordnance, rations, and equipment were stored in its rear. The army had only to await the right moment to show its power. In April, 1862, that time came. The sun dried the muddy Virginia roads. McClellan mounted his great black charger, Daniel Webster, and rode south at the head of his splendid army.

"On to Richmond!" was the battle cry as the sunburned men broke camp and marched forth singing "John Brown's Body" and "The Battle Hymn of the Republic."

Dolph swung along at the head of his squad, covering the miles with an easy stride. Glancing to the rear, he glimpsed the columns of men strung out for miles. Behind them rolled supply wagons, ambulances, and ammunition carts. Cavalry streamed past. Countless artillery batteries rattled on the rough-surfaced roads. Dozens of regimental, brigade, divisional, and corps flags fluttered brightly in the sun. Nobody, Dolph believed, could stand up to this great force.

But wars were not won by troops marching in precise formations behind snapping banners. Victory would come only after bitter fighting. General McClellan hurled his army against General Joe Johnston and the Confederate Army of Northern Virginia.

The armies met in bloody fights.

They clashed at Glendale, Gaines' Mill, and Fair Oaks, where Johnston was wounded and replaced by Robert E. Lee. The fighting went on without a respite. They fought at rivers and in forests, on farmland and mountain, in swamps and fields. At last the Northerners were beaten back from the outskirts of Richmond, and the Army of the Potomac retreated.

A Bad Blow

The Nineteenth Massachusetts was no longer made up of raw recruits. From its colors hung battle streamers: Malvern Hill, Petersburg, Yorktown, and Williamsburg—streamers which had cost many lives. The regiment had suffered heavily in the fighting and the men who had come through were now tough and canny veterans. War was an evil to Dolph. He hated the wasted lives and the destruction; but he believed in the struggle to preserve the Union, feeling that no sacrifice was too great to achieve that aim.

He also saw that war brought something besides death and devastation. Despite all the ruin and the misery, progress was resulting from the war. The needs of warfare presented a challenge, and men rose to face the challenge—not only with weapons but also with ideas.

For instance, railroads had never before been used on such a huge scale—daily, thousands of men and tons of freight rumbled over the tracks. New methods had to be developed in order to handle such volume. Engineers achieved wonders. They built miles of track in record time and learned to bridge deep gorges almost overnight. Track laying was brought to speedy perfection with new techniques for running roads across marshland and through forests.

Railroaders experimented in ways they would not have dared, nor even thought of, in peacetime. In order to carry greater loads, trains were twice and even three times longer than those in ordinary use. Two and three locomotives were used to haul the cars at speeds which were astonishing for that day —a locomotive usually averaged thirty-five miles an hour, but under war conditions it did fifty miles an hour and even better.

Dolph saw changes on every hand. Each day the New England farm boy witnessed marvels he would not have believed possible. Off Hampton Roads, Virginia, he saw the ironclad warship *Monitor* riding at anchor after its battle with the Confederate ironclad *Merrimac*—and, looking at the "cheesebox on a raft," Dolph knew he was having a peek at the future. The encounter between the ironclads had doomed forever the wooden warships and cleared the way for the great transatlantic ocean liners yet to come.

Dolph had another glimpse into the new world which was being fashioned by the war. A new element was brought into warfare during the fighting before Richmond. There Dolph witnessed the most imaginative of all Civil War experiments. A scientist, Professor Thaddeus Lowe, had for several years been making ascensions in lighter-than-air balloons. He convinced General McClellan to let him go up in a gas-filled silken bag and spy on the Rebels from above.

Lowe's first reconnaissance proved so successful that he made many other trips in his captive balloon—the *Intrepid*. He had a telegraph instrument with him and wired back much valuable information on the deployment of Confederate troops. He could, at a glance through his binoculars, see more ground than even the best cavalry scouts were able to cover in a week—and without danger from the enemy.

However, the conservative men in the War Department stubbornly refused to concede that Lowe's balloon had any military value.

"Cavalry has always been employed for scouting purposes and always will be. The professor's balloon is a mere toy unsuited for consideration by sober-minded men. Let the professor take his playthings elsewhere. They are not wanted in the United States Army!" a War Department spokesman sneered.

With official disapproval so openly expressed against the balloonist, Lowe's supporters, including General McClellan, deserted him. As a result, the professor was forced to disband his specially trained ground crews, deflate his balloons, and leave the Army of the Potomac—the target of ridicule from narrow-minded men, instead of the recipient of deserved praise.

Dolph was fascinated by Lowe's attempts to carry war into the air. He thought often about the balloons soaring high above the ground and wondered how it felt to ride in one.

"Sure must be great to soar like a bird," he mused one night while seated at a campfire with a group of Company D men who were discussing Professor Lowe's "gasbags," as the soldiers called the balloons.

"Ah, Corporal, there ain't anything to those geegaws. Now that Lowe's gone, nobody'll ever hear about him or his gasbags again. It ain't natural, anyway—if man was meant to fly, the Good Lord would've given him wings," a soldier scoffed.

"Oh, I don't know," Dolph said. "I think someday folks'll actually travel in airships far bigger than Lowe's balloons."

"You've been up on the lines too long, Corporal! The only way the likes of us will ever fly is when we sprout our angel wings, which ain't liable to happen," another soldier laughed.

Dolph jumped to his feet. "That's the trouble with you people! You're always ready to poke fun at new ideas! Folks called Robert Fulton a madman—but we have steamboats, don't we?"

"It ain't the same, Corporal," the first soldier argued. "Steamboats make sense, but flying in airships—"

Big Sven Petersen sat up lazily. "What's the point of all this talk? There's a war to be fought—and we'll be lucky to live through it, much less to see a world where folks will go gadding about in airships." He spat out a stream of tobacco juice and the men fell silent, thinking about the uncertain times that stretched before them.

Besides his interest in the balloons, Dolph showed great curiosity about the work of the United States Signal Service, which was in charge of all military communications. Prior to the Civil War, messages from field commanders to units in action were handled solely by runners or mounted messengers. In fact, cavalrymen spent most of their

A Bad Blow

time carrying dispatches when not scouting and patrolling.

However, several years before the war, in 1855, the Signal Service was established. Messages were sent by semaphore—a visual method employing special flags or lights. Men, trained for the purpose, wigwagged with signal flags, using a code in which the position of the flags indicated specific letters. At night, torches were waved from signal platforms in accordance with a code.

A military telegraphic bureau was also set up, but not too widely used. At the outbreak of the Civil War the Telegraphic Bureau was regarded as less important than the semaphore sections of the Signal Service. However, it was soon realized that visual signaling had grave drawbacks. The flags could be seen for only relatively short distances— and not at all after dark. Signaling by torch had the same fault, and it took a long time to transmit even a simple message by either method.

Telegraph communications could be sent over long distances and with great speed. As a result, higher headquarters were linked by telegraphic circuits. Commanders of armies were connected to each other and with the War Department by telegraph networks operated under the direction of the Signal Service. Messages which might have taken hours or even days in transmission by other means sped over the wires in minutes. President Lincoln and Secretary of War Edwin Stanton could communicate with their top generals speedily and easily, even though they were hundreds of miles apart. But at the front, contact between units was still maintained by couriers and visual signaling.

Whenever he had the chance, Dolph watched the Signal Service telegraphers at work. He learned from them the best way to string wire, and how to repair broken lines. He made friends among the dispatchers, who taught him the Morse Code, and he soon became expert in sending and receiving messages.

In 1862 a man who could "tickle a telegraph key" was both well paid and highly regarded. Because operating a telegraph-sender required so much skill and knowledge, a serious shortage of well-trained men developed. As a result, the military Telegraphic Bureau had to hire hundreds of civilian dispatchers to run its widespread networks; for it would have taken many months to train sufficient soldiers to do the work.

Although subject to military law, the operators were not actually mustered into the army but were often exposed to the same dangers as the troops. Many times telegraphers had to pick up rifles and beat off attacks by Confederate raiders.

Dolph frequently visited a scrawny, undersized operator named Seth Casey who had charge of a telegraph station near the regimental headquarters of the Nineteenth Massachusetts. Casey liked Dolph and taught him a great deal about telegraphy.

The young soldier spent hours in Casey's tent watching him work his key. During lulls, when the instrument was still, they drank coffee and talked.

One night Dolph described the Ball's Bluff

A Bad Blow

disaster to Casey. The skinny man listened, lamplight flickering across his wizened face.

"Sure and that's the army for you," Casey growled. "Sending you poor lads off to certain death, when a single telegraph line in the right place could have prevented the slaughter."

"What do you mean?" Dolph asked.

"If your commanders had known the situation at Ball's Bluff, they'd have withdrawn the troops and tried other tactics, wouldn't they?"

"I suppose so," Dolph said. "Nobody knew the situation until it was too late."

Casey shook his finger at Dolph. "If I was General McClellan, which I ain't, I'd have a telegraph unit attached to every company in the army. Fast as I dug my rifle pits, I'd have wire laid to regimental headquarters—and from there to division and all the way back to old Abe Lincoln himself." Casey pounded his table. "Then, by thunder, nobody'd have to guess what was happening! They'd know what was what all the time!"

"You're right, Casey!" Dolph cried. "We had no communications at Ball's Bluff—not even signal flags."

"Signal flags!" Casey snorted. "Now what earthly use are they? Look at your Signal Service—it's a joke. Those fellows waving their silly flags and torches. You can't see flags at night, and you can't see torches very far—or even read the messages plain. But the telegraph—ah, now, that's a different horse." Casey bit the end off a long cigar and struck a match. "Sure. They use telegraphers—but not right up front where we're needed. Tell me, how do you send messages back from the lines?" He puffed on the cigar, sending up a cloud of smoke.

"You know, Casey—by mounted couriers and runners," Dolph said.

"Couriers and runners. Same as in the days of Julius Caesar's legions! A man is shot, or falls off his horse, or gets lost. Then where is your message?"

"That happens all the time," Dolph smiled.

"Mark me, lad. Someday they'll see the Signal Service is more important than the whole blamed army put together. Because the army's blind without communications—and an army that don't know what it's doing can't fight. This is 1862! It's plain stupid to fight a war the same as they did in 1812—and my Grandpa, before that, during the Revolution!"

The key began chattering. "No rest for the weary," Casey sighed. He picked up a pencil and took the message as it came over. When he was done, he looked up at Dolph. "Lee crossed the Potomac at United States Ford. He's marching into Maryland. There's going to be a big fight."

Dolph rose. "I'd better get back, Casey. Thanks for the coffee and the talk."

"You're welcome, lad." Casey gripped Dolph's arm. "Be careful, boy."

"I'll do that," Dolph promised.

He stepped from the telegraph tent. Off to the

A Bad Blow

west, in the Maryland mountains, artillery grumbled. Dolph listened for a moment. "There'll be a big do," he muttered. "A real big one."

A week later, on September 17–18, the Army of the Potomac fought a tremendous battle with the Army of Northern Virginia at the sleepy Maryland town of Sharpsburg, on the shores of Antietam Creek. Never before had such a battle been joined on American soil. Thousands fell dead and wounded on both sides. Neither McClellan nor Lee won a clean-cut victory—but when the shooting finally died away, the Southern army limped back across the Potomac and withdrew from Northern soil.

The Nineteenth Massachusetts took part in the worst of the fighting around a place called "Bloody Lane" because of the many soldiers killed there in violent attacks and counterattacks. During one such charge Dolph had been struck in the jaw by a spent bullet which knocked out several of his teeth and broke his jawbone. At the same time another ball drilled his right leg through the calf.

He managed to drag himself back to a medical dressing station where he was given first aid and then sent to the big United States Military Hospital in Harrisburg, Pennsylvania.

For six weeks. Dolph stayed in the hospital, his jaw wired and his head and neck held in traction by splints. The days passed painfully, for the jaw healed with agonizing slowness; but at last the damaged bone knit and, on a crisp November day, the splints were removed. His leg wound had been a clean one which healed rapidly. Now he was waiting to be released from the hospital, eager for a return to duty.

During his stay in the hospital Dolph learned that the Nineteenth Massachusetts had suffered comparatively few casualties, thanks to the hard training and combat experience which made it one of the best units in the Army of the Potomac.

He had heard good news about his friends: Petersen had been cited for capturing the colors of an Alabama regiment, and Harris had been promoted to second lieutenant for bravery on the battlefield.

The hospital was daily growing more irksome to Dolph. He became moody and irritable, and sometimes felt he would never be allowed to leave. But, at last, Major David Marker, the medical officer commanding the hospital, examined him and announced, "Well, Corporal, I don't think you'll be able to chew hardtack for a while, but you're fit enough for duty. You may return to your regiment today."

"That's what I've been waiting to hear, Major," Dolph grinned.

"A real fighting cock, are you? Well, just see to it we don't have to patch you up again," Marker laughed. "I'll let you know when your discharge papers are ready and transportation back to your unit has been arranged."

The hours dragged. Dolph spent the morning pacing the ward. The other patients jeered at him for showing his desire to leave the hospital.

A Bad Blow

"Don't be in such an all-fired sweat, Corporal. The war won't be over. You'll have your chance to be killed," a soldier said.

"General McClellan can't get along without him," another laughed.

A soldier on crutches hobbled up to Dolph. "That's it, ain't it, mate? Little Mac needs you to tell him how things ought to be done."

Dolph took their teasing good-humoredly. At noon a hospital orderly came into the ward with a freshly pressed uniform, which he gave to Dolph. "This is for you, Corporal. Get dressed and report to Major Marker right away. You can pick up the rest of your gear from the quartermaster."

Dolph dressed hurriedly. He shook hands with the men and strode down the long corridor to Major Marker's office.

"Come in," Marker called in response to Dolph's knock.

Dolph saluted and stood at attention. "At ease, Greely," the major said. He eyed Dolph for a moment. "Corporal—I'm afraid I have bad news."

"You mean I can't leave, sir?"

Marker shook his head. "No. It's about your mother—"

"My mother! I had a letter from her only yesterday. What is it, sir?" Dolph asked anxiously.

"A telegram just arrived for you. As you know, all telegrams addressed to enlisted men must pass through the post senior officer. It was my sad duty to read this message." He handed the form to Dolph.

Dolph read it quickly. Then, with tears blurring his eyes, he read it once again:

> NEWBURYPORT, MASSACHUSETTS
> November 1, 1862
>
> CORPORAL A. W. GREELY
> Military Hospital
> Harrisburg, Pennsylvania
>
> Your mother fatally injured yesterday. Killed instantly when buckboard overturned en route farm to town. Awaiting instructions.
>
> LAWRENCE TOWNSEND
> *Mayor*

Dolph stared at the paper in his hand. This said Ma was dead. He let it flutter to the floor. Ma was dead! A sob shook him, but he fought to hold back his tears.

"Sorry, Major," he said chokingly.

"I know you want to get home, Greely," the Major said in a gentle voice. "I've drawn up a two-week furlough to start immediately. If you need more time, telegraph me. When your leave is over, report to your regiment. You have my sincerest sympathy."

"Thank you, sir," Dolph said brokenly.

Marker rose from his seat. He put an arm around Dolph's shoulders. "You're a good lad, Corporal—a first-rate soldier. Now take my advice, boy. Go off somewhere alone and cry until you've no more tears."

Dolph stumbled from the room. The hallway was deserted. He leaned against the wall and wept for a long time.

· · · CHAPTER 6

The Young Lieutenant

DOLPH SLOSHED THROUGH FROZEN, ANKLE-deep Virginia mud. The January north wind bit through the leafless trees, chilling all it touched. Leaden rain clouds hung motionless in the sky. Even in his heavy overcoat Dolph shivered.

Smoky fires marked the regimental encampment. Off to the right, through barren woods, he could see the sluggish Rappahannock River. Huge chunks of ice drifted on the gray water. Wherever he turned, the outlook was equally dismal.

Dolph had rejoined the regiment late in November. He still found it hard to accept the fact that Ma was dead—almost two months now. Folks back in Newburyport had been kind, but sorrow was no longer a stranger there. Scarcely a home had not known mourning and on Main Street one saw young men hobbling on canes or dragging along on crutches. The war had finally struck hard in Newburyport.

The townspeople flocked to Frances Greely's funeral. Elihu Whitlock, pastor of the First Pres-

The Young Lieutenant

byterian Church, delivered the eulogy. Even dour Fred Krebs, the crusty New Englander who ran the Greely farm, wept at his words.

Later Krebs had come to Dolph. "Don't fret, boy. I'll keep the place going. When you came back from the war, you'll have the farm—all I ask for myself is keep and lodging."

Dolph touched the thin white scar that ran along his jawbone. "Thanks, Mr. Krebs. I appreciate what you want to do, but I'm not keeping the farm."

"Not keeping the farm?" Krebs cried.

"I'm returning to my regiment at once. I might not be so lucky next time. I've asked Mayor Townsend to find a buyer for the place. If I do come through the war, I'll have some money; but I couldn't stay on here with Ma gone."

"I reckon you know what you're doing, boy. But don't act hasty. A farm's something for a boy to hang onto. What'll you do after the war, Dolph?"

"I'm not sure, Mr. Krebs. That's a long way off. I might stay in the army."

"The army." Krebs shook his head. "I had a bellyful of the army in Mexico. Mebbe you'll change your mind about that too."

"I don't think so, Mr. Krebs. In any case I don't want the farm."

"Well, if you're dead set on selling"—Krebs scratched his beard—"no point letting a stranger get it, is there? I have a little money. I'll buy it, Dolph."

So Krebs bought the Greely farm and Dolph had

six thousand dollars deposited to his name in the Newburyport Bank—more money than he had ever seen. He returned to the regiment, and the war ground on.

He slipped and almost fell in the mud. Of all nights to be corporal of the guard! Maybe the boys huddled around the fires in the encampment were miserable and uncomfortable—but, compared to the outpost pickets, they were living in luxury. There was no comfort out there in the night at the riverside. Dolph muttered a curse because he had been chosen to make the rounds and check on the sentries.

Much had happened since his return from Newburyport. General McClellan no longer commanded the Army of the Potomac. President Lincoln had removed "Little Mac" on November 5. The new leader was General Ambrose Burnside, a hardworking but untalented officer who had accepted his elevation reluctantly, convinced he did not have the qualifications for top command. He soon enough demonstrated that he had estimated himself correctly.

In December, shortly before Christmas, Burnside ordered a mass attack across the Rappahannock River against the Confederates entrenched on the heights of Fredericksburg, Virginia. The assault ended in tragic failure. The Army of the Potomac had five thousand fatalities. It was at this time that the Southern commander, General Robert E. Lee, watching his men mow down the Union troops, had

The Young Lieutenant

commented, "It is fortunate that war is so terrible, else we might grow too fond of it." The Nineteenth Massachusetts took part in the assault. Dolph had escaped unhurt, but Sven Petersen had been killed on the heights and Waldo Harris captured by the Rebels.

There were so few of the original volunteers left. Dave, Sven, Captain McCall, Willie Brierly, fifty others all dead. Waldo Harris in Libby Prison or on Belle Island. And no end to it. Nothing ahead but more and more fighting. Who would be there to see the end of the last battle?

Dolph shuddered in the cold darkness. He was doomed along with the rest, the pinch-faced, bearded young men who had seen too much pain and suffering and dying. The war would crush them all.

He stopped and turned his face up to the unfriendly sky. It started to rain. He shook himself and walked on, floundering from guard post to guard post, making sure the sentries were alert and knew their orders.

He finally came back to the guard tent and stumbled to the Sibley stove to warm himself. The duty officer, a young lieutenant newly arrived at the front, called to him, "Corporal Greely, report to Colonel Fischer at once." The lieutenant clipped his words, trying hard to sound sharply military.

"Oh, Lord—what does he want?" Dolph groaned from his place at the stove. Steam was rising from his wet clothing. An icy rain thrummed against the tent walls.

"I don't know, Corporal. Do you make a habit of questioning orders?" the lieutenant demanded.

A man lying in the shadow cut in. "Hey, shoulder strap! You're addressing a front-line hero. You read the newspapers, don't you? That's what they said we were—heroes! So how about some respect?"

Laughter exploded in the tent. The officer swung around. "I order the man who said that to show himself," he cried.

"Forget it, sonny! We may all be dead tomorrow. So feel lucky if you get off with only your feelings hurt," a soldier said.

"This is downright insubordination!" the lieutenant cried.

Dolph stepped up to him quickly. "I'm sorry, sir. I'll report to the colonel immediately. I was cold and tired. I've just come in from checking the outposts."

"Don't you think I know that, Corporal? This may be my first week out here, but I know what's going on. These men—is there no discipline in this regiment?"

"Yes, sir. Where it really matters—on the battle line. I'm afraid we left our good manners all the way from Ball's Bluff to the heights across the river. Some of us have been fighting for two years. I'll go to Colonel Fischer now, sir."

Dolph went into the rain and headed for the command post deep in the woods. He felt sorry for the lieutenant and his rear-echelon airs. He had probably been ordered into the field from a soft

The Young Lieutenant

desk job in Washington, where everyone was polite; where no one was hungry, cold, or scared. Well, Dolph thought, if the lieutenant lived long enough, he would learn.

The sentry at the command post told Dolph to go right in. "The Old Man's expecting you," the soldier said. He bared his teeth in a grin. "You're getting to be a mighty high muckety-muck, Mr. Greely—calling on the colonel, no less."

Inside, the stove was glowing pleasantly. A hissing carbide lamp gave off bright white light. Fischer was at a field desk, rustling through a sheaf of papers.

"Corporal Greely reporting as directed, sir," Dolph said.

"At ease, my boy." The colonel gestured toward a stool. "Sit down, Greely. I want to have a talk with you."

"Yes, sir." Dolph sat, wondering what the colonel had in mind.

"Corporal, I'll not keep you in suspense. I've recommended you for a lieutenancy," the colonel said.

"A commission? Sir, I never—"

Colonel Fischer raised his hand. "I thought it best to keep it quiet until I had something definite. This came through today from corps." He slid a document to Dolph, who read it quickly.

"Sir, it's my commission! I'm a second lieutenant. An officer!" Dolph cried excitedly.

"Yes, Greely. You're one of us, now—a shoulder strap," Fischer chuckled.

"I—I thank you, sir!"

"You may not want to do so in the future." He tapped the insignia on his shoulder. "This eagle can be a bird of prey. The lives of eight hundred men are my responsibility. It's a heavy weight to carry." He shook his head. "Perhaps I've done you no favor, Greely. But, for better or worse, accept my congratulations. I know you'll be a first-rate officer."

"I'll try, sir."

"My boy, I hate to lose you; but they need line officers in the new regiments—especially one with your battle experience. You will leave in the morning on the steamer for Washington, where you will report to the War Department for assignment. Pick up your orders from the sergeant major." The colonel extended his hand. "Good-by, Lieutenant Greely. I wish you the best of luck."

Outside, Dolph stood thoughtfully in the rain. Somewhere distant artillery rumbled. Gun flashes flickered on the horizon. He looked around at the familiar smoky campfires, the rows of tents, and the sentries hunched against the downpour. There was no sense worrying what might happen next. He had learned that the future reveals itself a bit at a time. Life was a card game, and fate the dealer. He had to take the cards as they fell, and the best he could hope for was an honest shuffle.

• • • CHAPTER 7

Mission on the Border

AT THE END OF THE WAR, IN APRIL, 1865, Dolph had decided to stay in the army. He transferred from the volunteer to the regular army as a second lieutenant in the Thirty-sixth Infantry Regiment, after having obtained the volunteer rank of brevet major with the Eighty-first Colored United States Infantry.

That regiment, made up of Negroes—both former slaves and freemen—had been the one to which Dolph was originally sent when commissioned an officer.

Many such regiments were authorized by Congress in 1863, after the Emancipation Proclamation went into effect. Negroes enlisted by the thousands, eager to show their desire for freedom by fighting for it. While all noncommissioned officers in these regiments were Negroes, the commissioned officers were white men selected from qualified combat veterans. The candidates were closely questioned regarding their feelings about slavery by a board of military men, Congressmen, and leading citizens.

Only those with strong antislavery leanings were finally picked to lead the Negro soldiers.

Dolph's abolitionist background made him eager to serve with Negro troops. He was assigned to the Eighty-first Colored Infantry, then training at New Orleans, and remained with that regiment until the end of the war. The Eighty-first saw action in the closing phases of the Vicksburg, Mississippi, campaign and also participated in the capture of Port Hudson, Louisiana. The outfit was kept busy guarding railroad and supply lines and patrolling occupied territory.

When his application for a commission in the regular army was approved, Dolph left the regiment—but the Negro troops would not let him go without a show of their affection for him. A delegation of his soldiers called on Dolph and, after some embarrassed shuffling, presented him with a gold watch inscribed with his name and the regimental slogan WE FIGHT AS FREE MEN.

Dolph was deeply touched by this gift and, before departing, shook hands with every man in the regiment. He made a brief farewell speech, saying, in part, "It has been my privilege to serve with you and to know you as brave and loyal men. Your future will not be an easy one. There are many problems ahead, but I know you will face them with the same courage you have shown in the trials of the past."

The Thirty-sixth Infantry Regiment of the regular army, to which he had been assigned, was stationed at Fort Sanders, Wyoming, near the Colorado border. This was in the heart of the frontier territory—rugged, untamed country through which hostile Indians roamed and where outlaws hid from the authorities.

Dolph's orders had called for him to proceed by rail to Denver, Colorado, where an escort from Fort Sanders was to meet him. On June 25, 1865, after a tiring and difficult train journey, he alighted at the rickety depot in Denver. No one awaited him at the station. He stayed for two hours, but no escort showed up.

The station master, a gnarled old man, hobbled to him. "Ain't none of my business, soldier boy, but why are you hanging around here? Ain't another train due until tomorrow."

"I was to meet an escort from Fort Sanders," Dolph said.

The old man looked at him, startled. "Fort Sanders, is it? Tarnation, sonny—you ain't goin' to Fort Sanders. Ain't you heard?"

"Heard what?"

"Why, the Bannock Indians are on the warpath. Them soldiers are buttoned up tight in the fort. They ain't expecting any visitors," the old man snickered.

"Well, I must get there," Dolph said. "Indians or no Indians." He picked up his carpetbag. "Where can I buy a horse?"

"A horse? Sonny, it's near one hundred and fifty miles to Fort Sanders, and every foot of the way through Indian country. You'd never make it and keep your hair. That scalp of yours'll be hanging from a Bannock lance before you've traveled twenty miles," the station master said.

"I appreciate the warning, old-timer. Now tell me where I can buy a horse," Dolph smiled.

"Morrison's livery stable, just down the street."

"Thanks." Dolph walked away, a trim figure in his uniform. He wore a full beard now and steel-rimmed eyeglasses, which added to his dignity.

He bought a sturdy horse, a suit of trail clothes —wide-brimmed Stetson, wool shirt, and buckskin pants—tied the carpetbag to his pommel, placed his carefully folded uniform in the saddlebags, strapped his army pistol to his waist, slipped a carbine in the saddle boot, and rode out.

Dolph was on the trail for three days and two nights. Once he spotted a group of Bannock warriors watching him from high ground, but they made no move toward him and he rode on to Fort Sanders unmolested.

Colonel William Bigelow, the commander of the Thirty-sixth Infantry, stared in disbelief when Dolph told of his travels through Indian country.

"Great Scott, man! Why in thunder did you come without an escort? You're lucky the Bannocks didn't make mincemeat out of you."

"I had to take that chance. I was expected here, and so I came. I've never yet shirked an order," Dolph said.

"Greely, I'm mighty pleased to have a man like you in my regiment," the colonel said. "And now that you're here," he added, "get into proper uniform. I don't allow my officers to dress like saddle tramps!"

The Thirty-sixth Infantry, under Colonel Bigelow, saw much active duty. In three years the regiment campaigned against the Bannock, Sioux, and Cheyenne tribes. Dolph learned much about Indian fighting.

He was pleased with his assignment to the regiment, for among the services it performed was one which he considered highly important. The Thirty-sixth guarded the Overland Mail route, which ran for five hundred miles from Fort Bridger, Wyoming, to Salt Lake City, Utah. This was a vital link in frontier communications—the only mail route to that part of the country.

Dolph learned to love the West—the great mountains, the sprawling prairie, and the trackless desert. But in 1868 a change took place in the United States Army which brought him out of the West for a long time. The United States Signal Service was reorganized to form a separate branch of the service as the United States Signal Corps under the command of General Albert James Myer, who had been in charge of the old Signal Service.

As an independent branch, the Signal Corps launched an expansion program. Qualified officers and enlisted men were given permission to apply for transfer to the corps. Dolph had never forgotten the prediction made by Seth Casey, the telegrapher, that one day the most important work in the army would be that done by the Signal Service;

but the telegrapher had not foreseen that only three years after the war a corps would be set up.

Dolph immediately advised Colonel Bigelow that he intended to file a request for transfer to the new organization.

"I belong in the Signal Corps, sir. I feel that the government would benefit most if I served there," he said.

Bigelow cleared his throat. "Well, Greely, by George, you're a first-class infantry officer—but, if you want to fool around with wires and batteries and such stuff instead of soldiering in a real outfit like the Thirty-sixth, I won't stand in your way. I'll approve the transfer and forward it to the War Department."

A month later the answer came to Fort Sanders in a terse War Department order:

> WAR DEPARTMENT
> WASHINGTON, D.C.
> *May 12, 1868
>
> 2nd Lt. A. W. Greely, assigned 5th Cavalry for administrative purposes and placed on permanent detached service with the U.S. Signal Corps. 2nd Lt. A. W. Greely will report to Commanding Officer, U.S. Signal Corps at Fortress Monroe, Virginia, without delay by first available transportation.
>
> EDWIN M. STANTON
> *Secretary of War*

Mission on the Border

But the day Dolph was to leave Fort Sanders an Indian uprising broke out and his departure was delayed several weeks. He finally reached Fortress Monroe late in July and reported to General Myer, who eyed him dourly.

"I was expecting you last month, Lieutenant. Since my table of organization allows me only ten junior officers, your place has already been filled. The Signal Corps has nothing for you just now," the general growled.

For a moment Dolph lost his military composure. His face showed his disappointment. "I couldn't get away because of the recent trouble on the frontier, sir, and, with all the wires down, there was no way to contact you. I came as soon as I could."

Myer locked his hands behind his back and scowled. "You have a fine military record, Mr. Greely, and I'd like to use you, but the question is where."

"It doesn't matter to me, General. I want to be in the Signal Corps—"

"Wait!" Myer snapped his fingers. "Do you know anything about meteorology? Weather prediction —that sort of thing?"

Dolph shook his head. "No, sir."

"Never mind, my lad. How would you like to be chief of the United States Weather Bureau?"

"The Weather Bureau?" Dolph gasped.

"I don't wonder at your surprise," Myer chuckled. "You see, in addition to our other duties, the Signal Corps has been made responsible for operating the Weather Bureau. The Bureau chief calls for a second lieutenant—and the post is open."

"But, sir, I don't qualify—"

"Fiddlesticks, Mr. Greely. The job is purely an administrative one. Three army meteorologists do the actual work. It's an easy assignment."

"I'm not looking for anything easy, General Myer."

"Very well, then. Listen to me. Right now the Weather Bureau is a farce. Nobody pays attention to the bulletins, the predictions, or anything else coming from that office. Storm warnings are ignored. Farm crops are destroyed by sudden changes of weather. Shipping suffers. Communications are disrupted and even lives lost, not to mention property damage, all because we lack a good weather service. You can build the Bureau into an important public function."

"I don't know anything about it. Not the first thing!" Dolph said unhappily.

"You can learn! You weren't a soldier before you joined the army," Myer snapped. "The post is open. I can always find a chair-warmer to take it. I'd prefer a man with backbone enough to face the challenge. What about it, Mr. Greely?"

"I've never run from anything in my life, sir. When do I start?" Dolph smiled.

• • • CHAPTER 8

The Weather Bureau

DOLPH REPORTED TO HIS NEW POST AS chief of the Weather Bureau the following day. The Bureau observatory was located high up in a tower of Fortress Monroe. Dolph climbed the winding stairs feeling like a man about to enter a prison cell.

"It was far worse than Ball's Bluff," he later said. "I was scared and unsure of what I would have to face. But duty was duty and I had accepted the assignment. I was determined to do a good job—even if I didn't quite know what was expected of me."

The observatory door was open and Dolph paused on the threshold of a large room cluttered with various pieces of meteorological equipment— barometers, thermometers, and similar devices. One wall was covered by a huge outline map of the United States. There were three soldiers on duty, each so completely engrossed in studying the instruments that no one noticed Dolph standing in the doorway. At last a burly, bearded private glanced up from his work.

"Yes, Lieutenant?" he asked. "Is there something we can do for you?"

"I hope so," Dolph smiled. "I'm Lieutenant Greely."

"Oh!" the private gulped. "The new boss." He turned to his companions. "Rice! Woodson! On your feet! It's the lieutenant!"

The two men jumped up. Dolph stepped into the room. "At ease," he said. "Which one of you is Private Francis Long?"

"I am, sir," the bearded soldier said. "That's Private George Rice and the other is Private Ben Woodson, sir. We're the U.S. Weather Bureau," he grinned.

Dolph looked about. "I see. And where do I work?"

"In there." Long pointed to a cubicle with a battered desk and a chair. The desk was all but buried under an untidy heap of papers. Dolph peered into the office.

"Not very grand, is it?" he said.

"No, sir," Long agreed. "But then the Weather Bureau isn't so much, either—if you don't mind my saying it."

"I don't mind, Private Long. It's the truth. General Myer gave me a black picture of this establishment. I'm going to try to change things. I'll need your help."

"Well, sir," Rice said, "we'll do whatever we can. The three of us are meteorologists—and darned good ones too. But it's no satisfaction for

The Weather Bureau

a man to do his job well and have nothing come of his efforts."

"The country needs this weather bureau, Lieutenant," Ben Woodson declared. "Yet we're hamstrung—shunted off like stepchildren; not enough room, not enough equipment, not enough funds!"

Long nudged Ben Woodson with his elbow. "Gentle down, soldier. No point in getting all excited."

"I'm sorry," Woodson said. "But when I think of the good we might do—and, this way, we're all of us wasting our time."

"That's what I mean to stop in the future," Dolph cut in. "I'd like you men to tell me what you think a weather bureau should do, how it can be of the most benefit to the public, and what must be done to build such an organization."

The three meteorologists exchanged glances. Long tugged at his beard thoughtfully. "Lieutenant Greely, I don't want to step out of line—but I must ask this question. You're not just—well—just sounding off, are you? Do you mean what you said?"

"I've never meant anything more in my life. I can understand how you men must feel about me. I'm a newcomer who knows nothing about the science of meteorology. But I intend to do something about that too. Which of you will volunteer to be my teacher?"

"I will!" the three soldiers cried together.

"Since there's no way to choose, you can all take turns—and maybe with the help of the three of you I'll become a meteorologist. Meanwhile get together and draw up a full report which will give me your picture of an ideal weather bureau—list the equipment you need, and the funds you feel are necessary. Then we'll see what happens."

Ben Woodson smiled widely. "You know something, lads—I have a feeling that we're coming out of the doldrums, and that we'll soon be sailing along before a fair breeze."

The days and weeks that followed were busy ones for Dolph. He learned the routines and procedures of the Bureau, whose function seemed limited to local weather observations and the compiling of charts and graphs showing wind velocity and coastal conditions based on facts submitted by Coast Guard observatories which telegraphed daily reports from various points along the Atlantic Coast. Since the Weather Bureau did not have its own telegraphic equipment, this data came through the Signal Corps message center and was often so delayed in delivery to the Bureau office that it no longer had any value.

Dolph also was kept occupied learning the fundamentals of meteorology. Woodson, Long, and Rice took turns showing him how to read a gravity barometer, a precipitation gauge, and an anemometer, which recorded wind velocities. They taught him to observe and recognize cloud formations, the different types of clouds, and the visual signs that indicated changes in weather. He was a good pupil and soon became a capable weatherman.

At the same time the three men labored over the lengthy and detailed report which he had re-

The Weather Bureau

quested. At last it was completed. Dolph leafed through the pages.

"Good work, lads," he said. "Let me study this awhile and then I'll see what I can do to put your plan into action."

The report gave a detailed analysis of how the Bureau should be operated. Dolph liked what he read. It was suggested that weather observatories manned by competent and qualified personnel be established at key points throughout the country and linked to the central office in Washington by telegraph. Every twelve hours each sub-Bureau would wire in its summary of local weather conditions. Warnings of blizzards, floods, heavy rains, and other disturbances would be posted in affected areas.

Special bulletins were to be issued at regular periods to advise farmers of expected weather during planting and harvesting seasons. Coast Guard stations were to submit climatic conditions to the Washington Bureau at twenty-four-hour intervals, and all harbor masters in major ports would be kept informed of any anticipated storms so that this data could be passed on to the skippers of vessels about to sail.

The sub-Bureaus would issue weather bulletins to major daily morning newspapers in their districts and request that they be printed in early editions as a service to the public.

Dolph presented the report to General Myer in mid-September. A week later the general sent for him. "Greely, you've done a good job. The report by your men is fine. I'm sure you will be pleased to know I have approved it, and that the recommendations incorporated in it will be implemented. I have already requested a twenty-five-thousand-dollar appropriation for the purchase of necessary equipment to establish properly staffed sub-Bureaus. A Signal Corps telegraphic network for the sole use of the Weather Bureau will be made available to you."

Within a year the Weather Bureau was operating on a nation-wide scale. The central office was given a splendidly equipped new observatory in an unused warehouse at Fortress Monroe and Dolph's three-man crew had been increased to twelve.

In the spring of 1870 disastrous floods caused widespread damage throughout the Mississippi Valley. Dolph traveled to the ravaged area.

"Floods can be prevented," he insisted. He consulted with army engineers and evolved a program of flood control through the construction of levees and by dredging stream beds to carry the overflow of swollen rivers.

For the next three years Dolph applied himself to inspecting potential flood-danger areas. He presented a program that called for extensive dam- and dike-building projects, but economy-minded Congressional finance committees scuttled his plans.

"The politicians would rather save a few dollars in the name of economy than provide a means of saving lives, crops, homes, and eventually millions of dollars," he stated in disgust.

The Weather Bureau

During his fifth year with the now smoothly functioning Weather Bureau, he was summoned by General Myer in September, 1873.

"Greely, I have a new assignment for you," Myer said.

"I'm satisfied where I am, sir," Dolph replied.

"Mr. Greely—you've accomplished one mission. Now it's time to take on another. President Grant has ordered the Signal Corps to build a telegraph system linking all the forts in Wyoming. I believe you are familiar with that region?"

"I put in three years at Fort Sanders, sir."

Myer nodded. "That's why I've selected you to supervise the installation of those telegraph lines. You'll find working in the field a lot different from the Weather Bureau—"

"Yes, sir—but I'll have plenty of weather in Wyoming. I remember those blizzards in the mountains," Dolph said. He sighed wistfully. "I thought I'd left all that behind me—but you never know in the army, do you?"

General Myer handed Dolph a rolled-up map. "I want you to study this—the proposed route for the lines. They'll run about twelve hundred miles. And President Grant expects the job to be completed by March first, next year—which gives you six months. Good luck, Greely. You'll need it."

Dolph took the map. "I should have known it wasn't going to be easy," he laughed.

• • • CHAPTER 9

A Presidential Bet

DOLPH ARRIVED IN WYOMING EARLY IN October with a party of Signal Corps linemen and wiremen, and a detail of surveyors recruited from the Corps of Army Engineers. He hired a hundred civilian laborers and began to work putting up the telegraph line.

The surveyors went first, laying out the best route from point to point. They were followed by the laborers who felled and stripped trees, cutting them to the lengths needed for telegraph poles. Then the workmen set up the poles all along the way. The Signal Corps linemen and wiremen came on after the poles had been erected. Mules carried great spools of telegraph wire on their backs. The linemen scrambled up and down the poles, fastening the wire into place on the crossarms. The wiremen made the final splicing and installed the glass insulators around which each connecting wire was wound.

Dolph rode from one end of the trail to the other, making certain that the work was progressing on schedule and helping unsnarl any difficulties. There were plenty of problems. Supply wagons could not keep up with the swiftly moving wire parties, and this caused some delays. But Dolph's chief assistant, a seasoned Signal Corps regular, Sergeant Fred Milroy, kept the wagons rolling. Even a stubborn army mule moved when Milroy bellowed "Get going!"

Fortunately winter came late to Wyoming that year, with none of the usual blizzards to hamper the work. The tremendous task of stringing twelve hundred miles of telegraph wire in six months was accomplished on schedule. The last connection was coupled and spliced on March 1, 1874. Dolph tapped out the message:

TO ALL ARMY POST COMMANDERS IN WYOMING
THIS CIRCUIT IS NOW IN OPERATION THANKS
TO THE UNITED STATES SIGNAL CORPS

If he had held any hopes that finishing the Wyoming assignment on time meant an early return to Washington, they were soon dashed by an order from General Myer which sent Dolph and his men into Dakota Territory. Another telegraph line was to be constructed there—several hundred miles of wire through the Bad Lands, a desolate, mountainous region guarded by widely separated cavalry and infantry units which garrisoned a number of isolated forts. The purpose of this telegraph line was to enable these posts to communicate with one another.

As he had in Wyoming, Dolph pushed the mission to a successful conclusion. He had been in the field for nearly a year, but once again he was ordered to another job without respite.

This time he faced his most demanding assignment. A two-thousand-mile-long telegraph network was to be strung along the Texas-Mexican border following the course of the Rio Grande and reaching out to various army posts and stations. It was a task that had to be carried out under great odds. Dolph had been recalled to Washington to be briefed by General Myer. "Mr. Greely, I am aware of the difficulties which will confront you in Texas. You'll find no lumber there, a terrible climate, and potentially hostile Indians. Three other officers have failed to carry through this mission. But I have full confidence that you will succeed. I'm certain you understand the need for a telegraph line along the Mexican border."

Dolph fingered his beard. Just once, he'd have liked a simple assignment—but somebody had to do the rough ones. It had been the same during the war—the armchair soldiers in Washington had not won the victory. It had been gained by the troops in the field. And so it was that on a day in July, 1875, Dolph rode at the head of a column of horsemen across the Texas flatlands near the Mexican border. Ashy dust powdered the blue uniforms of the soldiers with a white film. Nothing broke the billiard-table flatness of the land or offered protection from the sun—no hill, no clump of trees could be seen in any direction. Except for sagebrush and stunted bushes, the region was nearly barren.

Dolph halted the riders and through field glasses

scanned the expanse behind him, searching for the six lumbering supply wagons following with reels of wire, tools, and equipment. At last he spied them. The huge wagons, each drawn by a twenty-mule team, were mere specks in the distance.

Dolph replaced his binoculars and mopped his bearded face with a bandanna. It was time to rest both riders and horses. He regretted that the men and animals had neither shade nor water, but this was the Texas border in July. Shade and water were hard to come by.

He signaled the men to dismount and swung stiffly down from his own horse. In seconds the soldiers were sprawling on the ground, eyes shielded from the sun by their wide-brimmed campaign hats. Dolph took a sip of the hot, brackish water in his canteen. He screwed the canteen cap on again, removed his silver-framed eyeglasses and carefully polished the lenses.

His chief assistant came to him. "How about this weather, Lieutenant?"

"We're in Texas, Sergeant Milroy." He finished cleaning his eyeglasses and put them back on. "Texas—an area of the country never noted for gentle summers."

"You can say that again, sir."

"Sergeant, let's not talk about the weather. I find it depressing. How much farther to our base camp?"

Fred Milroy shielded his eyes and peered into the shimmering heat waves. "Five, six miles.

Shouldn't take too long—that is, if those blasted supply wagons ever catch up with us."

"The mules are about played out hauling those loads." Dolph glanced around. "I've never seen such country. Heat, dust, and flies."

"Ain't you forgetting the Comanches, Lieutenant?"

"Ah, yes. The Comanches." Dolph sighed. "I hope we don't run into any."

"I was down here during the war, Lieutenant, chasing both Rebels and Comanches. We didn't mind tangling with Rebs—but Comanches!" He made a face. "Ugh. They're smart and mean. Best fighters I ever saw."

"So you've told me, Sergeant—a dozen times. You told me all about the Comanches last year in Wyoming and, after that, in Dakota Territory. I don't want anything to do with them. We've enough troubles on our hands as it is."

"You ain't just whistling, Lieutenant. The whole setup is loco, if you ask me! How do they expect us to string a thousand miles of wire along this blasted border?"

Dolph wagged a finger at the angry sergeant. "Now, now, Milroy—don't blow up!"

"I'm human, ain't I? Sure, we've strung wire all over Wyoming and Dakota—and that wasn't easy. But, by jiminy, we had trees for telegraph poles! Plenty of trees. Take a look, Lieutenant. No trees here. Only those runty bushes. What are we supposed to do for poles?"

"Sergeant, how long have you been in the army?" Dolph asked patiently.

"I joined in sixty-one."

"After fourteen years in the service, you must have learned that a soldier follows orders and keeps his mouth shut."

"Yes, sir," Milroy said. "But how're we going to do this job without telegraph poles?"

"We'll hit on something, Milroy. There's always a way," Dolph said confidently.

"If you say so, Lieutenant. But I still think—ah, what's the use? I ain't paid to think!" Milroy stalked off to join the other men.

After a while, when the wagons drew closer, Dolph mopped his brow with a kerchief. It was time to move on. At his command the men mounted and jogged to the base work camp which had been set up by an advance detail. Surveyors were sent out and soon had marked a route for the telegraph line—but the work came to a halt at that point.

Dolph scouted the country for miles, but could not find enough trees to make into telegraph poles. Days passed with the men lounging about the base camp with nothing to do.

"It's no use," Dolph announced to Sergeant Milroy. "I'm licked."

"It's a rotten shame, Lieutenant—but this whole deal was scuttled before we even started," Milroy growled.

"If only there were some trees in this forsaken country!" Dolph cried.

"Trees. By golly, sir, do you remember all the junipers growing up in Virginia near White Oak Swamp? Junipers—thousands of 'em. We sure could use those trees," Milroy said wistfully.

"Juniper trees. They'd do fine," Dolph murmured.

"You can say that again, sir. But there ain't any use dreaming. We don't have trees, nothing but scraggly bushes, and we're scalped—"

"The juniper trees! That's it! Milroy, we're going to be all right," Dolph laughed.

"Lieutenant, are you okay? You ain't been out in the sun too long?" Milroy asked in anxious tones.

"Of course not! You started me thinking, Sergeant. Why can't we have juniper trees—all we need—cut to size and trimmed in Virginia, then shipped by boat to Galveston? We'll haul them on wagons where they're wanted."

Milroy swept off his hat and bowed low. "Lieutenant, you're a genius! Pardon my saying so, but the idea is wild enough to work. You think General Myer will go along with you?"

"If he wants a telegraph line, he'll have to—unless he can think of a better solution. I'll write him tonight—and we'll sit and wait."

Myer approved the plan. In a few months ten thousand juniper trees from Virginia were carrying the telegraph wire all along the Texas–Mexican border.

On Dolph's return to Washington, in March, 1876, President Grant invited him to the White

A Presidential Bet

House for a private meeting. Chomping on a cigar, Grant studied the young officer.

"That was quite a stunt you pulled off down in Texas," the President beamed.

"Thank you, sir," Dolph said modestly. "I had some good men working with me."

"But shipping the juniper trees down from Virginia was your idea." Grant chuckled. "Juniper trees—that's a humdinger. Frankly we'd given up hope on that particular telegraph line. Believe me, Greely, had I been sent on such an assignment, I'd have thrown up the sponge. I never really believed you could do that job, so I bet General Myer twenty-five dollars that you'd fail. I was never more delighted to lose a bet!" Grant exhaled a cloud of smoke. "Juniper trees! By gosh, Greely, that was clear thinking. Juniper trees!"

• • • CHAPTER 10

The Lady Franklin Bay Expedition

DOLPH HAD BEEN IN THE FIELD ALMOST continuously for three years and in May, 1876, he applied for a three-month leave of absence. "Mr. Greely, I am turning down your leave application," General Myer told him.

"But, sir, I'm entitled to it," Dolph protested. "I've had no leave for more than thirty-six months, and—"

"Tell me, Mr. Greely, what did you intend to do with your leave?" the general asked.

"I hadn't quite made up my mind, sir. I have friends in New York I'd like to visit—"

General Myer smiled faintly, as though remembering a joke. "Mr. Greely, have you ever been to Europe?" he asked.

"No, sir. I've had a hankering to go abroad, but never had the opportunity."

"I see. You think me an ogre for refusing your leave, don't you, Mr. Greely?" Myer asked, his eyes twinkling.

The Lady Franklin Bay Expedition

"No—no, sir—I—I—" Dolph stammered. "I'm certain the general has his reasons—"

"I have, Lieutenant. There's a special mission I want you to do for the Signal Corps. It will take three months and require an ocean voyage."

"An ocean voyage, sir?"

"Yes. I thought it might be a good idea to send an officer to observe the Signal Corps of foreign armies in operation. Permission has been granted by the British, French, and Austrians. You are to be that officer!"

"General Myer! You mean I'm going to Europe!" Dolph cried. "General—I—I'm overwhelmed, sir—"

"Never mind that, my boy. Pack your bags and see to it that your dress uniform is packed. Our European colleagues go in for formal entertaining."

Dolph returned from his trip in September, 1876. It had been an exciting experience. The British, French, and Austrian armies boasted highly efficient Signal Corps. Their equipment was more advanced than that used by the United States, and Dolph had learned a great deal about signal operations. On his return to duty he wrote an exhaustive report on his observations and submitted it to General Myer, who praised him for the thoroughness of his work.

The general led him to a wall map of the United States. "I will now show you what your next job will be," he said.

Myer traced a route with his forefinger between Santa Fe, New Mexico, and San Diego, California.

"Mr. Greely, we want a telegraph line to connect these points. Work is already under way, but you are to go out there and complete it."

Dolph tried not to show his disappointment. He had been hoping for another sort of assignment. Building telegraph lines no longer was a challenge. He had already supervised the stringing of more than five thousand miles of wire.

General Myer noted the expression on Dolph's face. "What's the matter, Lieutenant?" he asked.

"Nothing, sir. I'll draw up the requisitions for supplies," Dolph said.

"I've known you nearly ten years, Mr. Greely." Myer smoothed his white mustache. "During that time you've made a fine record in the service and have done much for the Signal Corps."

"I've tried my best, General."

"I know what's bothering you, Mr. Greely. You've just returned from London, Paris, Vienna —the great cities of Europe—where you've seen much and mingled with important people, but now you're to head back out on the frontier. Quite a change from what you've seen these last few months."

"I'm a soldier, General. I go where I'm ordered."

"Sometimes orders are distasteful," the general said in a kindly voice. "Perhaps you're thinking that other officers are available for field duty. Perhaps you would like a chance to stay in Washington awhile. The truth is, I can't spare you from the field. You're a man who sees a job through—and such men are too rare these days."

"You didn't have to explain, sir."

"I wanted you to understand." Myer clapped Dolph on the shoulder. "This time you won't have to haul juniper trees from Virginia. You'll have all the supplies you need right at hand."

Work on the new telegraph line went quickly. By election day in November, a section of the circuit was in operation and the news that Rutherford B. Hayes had defeated Samuel Tilden for the Presidency of the United States, in a tight race, was flashed over the wires.

On December 24, 1876, Dolph declared the mission finished. From San Diego he wired a holiday greeting to Santa Fe. On Christmas Day a committee of prominent San Diego residents held a party for Dolph and his men. A tall, beautiful brunette, twenty-year-old Henrietta Nesmith, was among the guests. Dolph thought she was the prettiest girl he had ever seen—to his surprise he found himself in love.

But the army had little place for sentiment. A week after that Christmas party Dolph was ordered back to Washington. His chances of coming to San Diego again were slim, and he was determined not to lose Henrietta so he wired General Myer, asking a month's leave, with scant hope that his request would be granted. However, the general gave it to him. His telegram said, "This a slight favor for a job well done."

Wasting no time, Dolph launched a campaign to win Henrietta. He bombarded the girl with gifts, candy, and flowers. He took her to teas, dances, parties, and on buggy rides into the country.

One evening she said, "Dolph, you needn't try so hard to impress me. I'm already impressed. You see, I fell in love with you the first moment I ever saw you."

They were married before his leave was up. Dolph returned to Washington with his bride. For a time he did staff duty in Washington, but in 1878 there were Indian uprisings in Dakota Territory. He was ordered west once more to build another telegraph line—this one stretching all the way from Bismarck, North Dakota, to Oregon.

A year later he hurried home to Henrietta and was once more placed on General Myer's staff as an aide. In October, 1879, an event in Hamburg, Germany, changed the course of his life.

Ten countries—Norway, Sweden, Holland, Russia, Finland, the United States, England, Germany, Denmark, and Austria—sent delegates to an international conference held at Hamburg, for the purpose of setting up observation posts within the Arctic and Antarctic circles to explore and chart these regions and also to study meteorological conditions there. This was the first time a combined international effort was being made to investigate the polar regions.

Congress authorized United States participation in the circumpolar expeditions. Two American parties were to man stations—one at Point Barrow, Alaska; the other at Lady Franklin Bay, Grinnell Land, across Robeson Channel from northern Greenland.

The Lady Franklin Bay Expedition

The latter was the most northerly outpost of all. All groups were scheduled to be in position by August, 1881, and to remain there for a period of three years.

While all these arrangements were being carried out, Dolph remained in Washington. His old friend General Myer had retired on January 1, 1880, and the Signal Corps had a new commander, General William Babcock Hazen, who kept Dolph as his aide.

Dolph was now thirty-six years old. He had served nearly twenty years in the army. Now his life seemed to have settled into a comfortable routine. He was happy with Henrietta; they had two daughters—Antoinette, aged three years, and Adola, aged three months. Although still a first lieutenant, Dolph was satisfied with his career. Promotions came slowly in the army—especially in the Signal Corps, a comparatively new branch.

Early in March, 1881, General Hazen summoned Dolph. "You've heard about the circumpolar stations decided on two years ago at the Hamburg Convention, haven't you, Greely?" the general asked.

"Yes, sir. I'm only vaguely aware of their purpose—"

"Briefly the main reason for setting up such stations is to explore the Arctic regions, to study certain scientific and meteorological conditions that exist there—but mainly to determine how best to survive in such an extreme climate."

"I see, sir."

"The President has placed the Signal Corps in charge of the two stations which the United States is to operate. He has ordered me to select a man to lead the Lady Franklin Bay Expedition. I've made my choice," Hazen said. "That's why I sent for you."

"Yes, General?"

"You're that man, Mr. Greely!"

Dolph looked at his superior in confusion. "Me, sir? I know almost nothing about the Arctic. Surely there must be a better man—"

"Neither I nor President Garfield thinks there is. In the past, whenever the Signal Corps had a tough job to do, the slogan has been 'Let Greely Do It'—and we believe this is another such situation. Of course you may refuse the assignment, if you wish."

Dolph raised a hand in protest. "I didn't say that, sir. This is a great honor. But, frankly, I don't even know where to begin."

"The start has already been made. The President issued a call for volunteers from the army. You will have a complement of twenty-five men: two officers, twenty-two enlisted men, and a doctor. All the enlisted men will be either specialists or persons who have had experience in the Far North. They will include meteorologists, geologists, oceanographers, and so forth. Do you think you will be ready to start working on this project tomorrow?"

"Today, if necessary—" Dolph suddenly paused and looked troubled.

"Is something the matter, Greely?"

"Well, sir, I don't know how Mrs. Greely will feel about such an assignment. I believe the expe-

The Lady Franklin Bay Expedition

dition is expected to stay in the Arctic for three years."

"That's true, but Mrs. Greely is a soldier's wife. I'm certain she will take the news well. Report to me in the morning. There's much to be done. The expedition is scheduled to sail on July seventh, from Newfoundland."

"I'm ready, sir."

Hazen placed his hand on Dolph's arm. "I know what a hardship it is for a man to be separated from his family for so long a period. It would also be folly to underestimate the hazards you will face. You're as aware as I am of the fate that has overtaken other Arctic expeditions."

"I know, General." Dolph smiled at him. "I've been in danger before."

Henrietta listened calmly when Dolph explained his assignment. "The children and I will miss you, Dolph—but we shall be proud of you every moment you are gone."

The following weeks were filled with activity. Dolph worked until late every night poring over the maps and charts of Grinnell Land, far to the north of Baffin Bay. He studied the plans of the ship that would carry the party to Lady Franklin Bay. The choice was the *Proteus,* a sturdy, steam barkentine-rigged whaler. For protection against ice the vessel was to be sheathed with ironwood from her water line to below the turn of the bilge, and her bow armored with thick iron plate for icebreaking. This work was being done in a St. John's, Newfoundland, shipyard.

Dolph conferred frequently with General Hazen, reviewing every detail of the expedition. Meanwhile soldiers from all branches of the army were volunteering for the mission. After Dolph and Hazen had interviewed many applicants, the detachment was finally selected. The officers were Second Lieutenant Frederick F. Kislingbury, Eleventh Infantry, a former northwoods guide and trapper, and Second Lieutenant James B. Lockwood, Twenty-third Infantry, who had been a lumberjack in Oregon.

Among the enlisted men, Sergeant Edward Israel, Signal Corps, was not only a trained chemist but also a photographer. Sergeant David L. Brainard, Second Cavalry, was a map maker. Private Francis Long, Ninth Infantry, a meteorologist, had come from the Weather Bureau, as had Sergeant George Rice. Every enlisted man had been a woodsman, a hunter, or else had a scientific specialty. The doctor, Octave Pavy, a Canadian, had worked in the North, near Hudson Bay.

Hazen and Dolph often talked about the kind of shelter best suited for the party's needs, once it arrived at Lady Franklin Bay. Since the expedition was to stay for three years, some sort of semi-permanent building had to be constructed. Because not a stick of lumber was to be found in that desolate region, necessary materials would have to be hauled by the *Proteus*.

A problem facing Dolph and his men would be the time needed to erect the shelter. Many hours were spent discussing ways to save time in putting

The Lady Franklin Bay Expedition

it up, but neither Dolph nor the General could find a solution.

One morning Dolph burst into Hazen's office. "By George, I have it, General!" he cried.

"What are you talking about?" Hazen asked.

"The building, General. I've found a way, I think, to save us a lot of time. If all the planks are cut here and the sections fitted together, we can then take the building apart and reassemble it when we reach Lady Franklin Bay."

The general rubbed his chin. "Mr. Greely, that's a capital idea. Why, you should be able to get that building up in a jiffy. Go ahead, Lieutenant. You have my fullest approval."

Dolph put a team of architects to work. They soon had blueprints drawn—in a week the house was standing on the Fortress Monroe parade ground. A corps of carpenters had thrown it up in a few days. The house was sixty feet long and seventeen feet wide and was divided into three rooms—one for the officers, another for the enlisted men, and the third equipped as a kitchen and bathroom. The walls were made of double-thick one-half-inch board between which was left a twelve-inch air space to act as insulation. The outer walls and the roof were covered with tar paper for weatherproofing.

When the building was completed to Dolph's satisfaction, he had the workmen carefully dismantle it. The sections were clearly marked to speed up the reassembling work, and then crated. This was possibly the first prefabricated dwelling.

On June 15, 1881, an advance party of the Lady Franklin Bay Expedition left Washington for St. John's, Newfoundland, under command of Lieutenant Kislingbury. This detail supervised the loading of the *Proteus* with a two-year supply of provisions. The scientific equipment for the expedition—an anemometer to measure wind velocity, mercury thermometers, barometers, dew-point measuring devices, lead-lined containers for storing specimens of lichen moss and sea weed, and many additional pieces of apparatus—was hoisted aboard.

Crates of Arctic clothing, fur-lined parkas, pile-lined trousers, shoe pacs and other items of clothing, sleeping bags, rifles, pistols, tents, ammunition, books, and even musical instruments were lowered into the hold.

Dolph and the main body arrived in time for the ship to sail precisely on schedule—July 7, 1881. When the *Proteus* weighed anchor, morning mists swirled about her as she cleared St. John's harbor. Dolph stood leaning on the taffrail above the steam launch slung on special davits from the stern of the vessel. He stared back at the dimly seen shore line which lay shrouded in mist. Once the ship was riding the open sea, he ordered a meeting of officers and noncommissioned officers in his cabin.

When the men had assembled, he addressed them: "Gentlemen, the time has come to fill you in with all details of our mission. As you know, we are expected to remain at Lady Franklin Bay for three years. I am now authorized to inform you that anyone who so desires may return with the *Proteus* without prejudice to himself when she leaves this party at Lady Franklin Bay. Is there anyone who now wishes to take advantage of this offer?"

The men stirred uneasily, but no one spoke. Dolph grinned at them. "I take it that so far no one has a case of cold feet. Once we reach the Arctic, that situation may change."

A laugh went up from the group.

When his listeners had settled down, Dolph continued: "We are carrying enough food to last until August, 1883—but, each year of our Arctic stay, a ship will be sent to bring us supplies and mail. In case the first ship fails to contact us, she will leave our cargo at predesignated places along the east coast of Grinnell Land; namely, Cape Hawks, Cape Isabella, and Cape Sabine. We will send parties with sleds to bring in the supplies."

He paused and looked at the men. "Is this clear?"

"Yes, sir," voices replied.

"Very well," Dolph went on. "Should the 1882 ship arrive at Lady Franklin Bay, the 1883 ship will make a similar effort. If she does not succeed, she will remain at anchor in Smith Sound until there is danger of being shut in by ice. We will send sled teams out to find the ship. Should the ship be forced to leave before contacting us, she will land her supplies plus a party prepared for a winter's stay. This group will proceed to Lady Franklin Bay by sled, traveling up the east coast of Grinnell Land."

Dolph folded his arms across his chest. "That's it, gentlemen. Are there any questions?"

Lieutenant Kislingbury raised his hand. "Sir,

what if no ship comes either in 1882 or 1883? It is also possible that we may not be able to locate the supplies left for us."

Dolph stroked his beard. "That would be an extreme situation indeed, Mr. Kislingbury. However, I have orders to retreat from Lady Franklin Bay if no vessel reaches us by August, 1883. We will move down the east coast of Grinnell Land to await a rescue ship at Cape Sabine. It should arrive there in the summer of 1884. As for not finding the supplies that will be left for us—I can only say that, while every measure has been taken to ensure our safe return, we are, as always, in the hands of God."

After several other questions the meeting was adjourned. The men filed out of the cabin and Dolph sat alone. He stared at the maps spread on the table and rested his finger on the pinpoint called Lady Franklin Bay.

• • • CHAPTER 11

The Last Outpost

FOR DAYS THE PROTEUS STEAMED STEADILY northward through gray waters under a bleak sky. Although she had sailed from Newfoundland in midsummer, the winter was already starting in the Arctic. The north wind slashed like a whip. It howled at night and, in the darkness, the men on watch drew their fur-lined parkas tighter.

Soon ice floes were sighted in the thick fog banks that hung over the water. The *Proteus* slowed to avoid collision with the towering ice. But, despite the wintry signs, there was still clear water and the ship was able to continue on its way.

After a week at sea Dolph faced his first command problem of the voyage. Some deck cargo had been poorly lashed in place and, during a wind storm, the crates shifted and were nearly washed overboard. Dolph rebuked Lieutenant Kislingbury, who had been in charge of loading the vessel, for his oversight in not checking the ropes.

Kislingbury, a hotheaded man, grew angry at Dolph's scolding. "I want to be relieved of duty with this mission, sir," he said. "It's my privilege."

"Of course, Mr. Kislingbury. But there is nothing I can do for you now," Dolph smiled, hoping to calm the young officer. "Unless you'd care to swim back."

"I insist on being relieved," Kislingbury said coldly.

"You may return aboard the *Proteus,* Lieutenant—but in the meantime I expect you to carry out your duties. You are not relieved until I have given you written orders to that effect," Dolph stated.

Although Kislingbury did his job well, he remained unfriendly toward Dolph and his attitude clouded the balance of the trip.

The *Proteus* followed the west coast of Greenland into Baffin Bay. A stop was made at Godhavn, an Eskimo settlement on the Danish-owned island of Disko, where Dolph bought sleds and dog teams. He also hired two native hunters, Frederick Thorley Christiansen and Jens Edwards. The men were expert guides and had accompanied other Arctic expeditions. After completing this business, Dolph ordered the *Proteus* out to sea again.

He was in his cabin on the morning of August 4, 1881, when the crow's nest lookout cried "Land Ho!" Dolph hurried up on deck. His men were crowding the port rail, peering through the mist toward a head of land. Dolph studied the snow-covered wastes through his binoculars. "Well, boys," he announced, "we are at Lady Franklin Bay."

A cheer crackled in the icy air. The *Proteus* had safely finished her voyage. Now they were four

The Last Outpost

hundred and ninety-six miles south of the North Pole and two hundred and fifty miles farther north than Etah, the most remote Eskimo village. Lady Franklin Bay was the last outpost in the world.

Dolph put his men to work unloading the ship. It was a laborious task. The *Proteus* could not approach closer than a quarter of a mile from shore because a solid ice field extended that far into the bay. All supplies and equipment had to be dragged ashore on sleds or hand-hauled over the ice mass. In the meantime the temperature dropped and by nightfall the thermometer had readings of fifteen to twenty degrees below zero. Gales swept from inland, but the work went on.

It was soon evident they had to face the bad weather that was closing in. The *Proteus* was in danger of being trapped in the ice which had started to form on all sides of the ship. If the vessel did become ice-locked, it could be pinched between cakes of ice which closed with tremendous pressure crushing anything caught between like a giant pincers.

The men worked without rest and with little food. By August 10, according to the journal kept by Sergeant David Brainard:

> The last supplies have been set ashore. We are now fitting the house together. These past days we have been sheltered in tents and sleeping bags. The cold is terrible, but we are growing accustomed to it. The ship is pretty well

stuck in the ice. But she is a tough old scow and will try to break her way out, very soon.

By midday, August 11, the house was set up. Privates Julius Fredericks and Henry Biederbeck, both good cooks, took over the kitchen. They soon had the kerosene cookstove glowing red and the men mopped up their first hot meal in the Arctic.

The steam launch, promptly christened the *Lady Greely*, was dragged ashore and three of the *Proteus'* lifeboats were also hauled to land. With an American flag in his hand Dolph called the men together. A flagpole had been fixed to the roof of the house.

"This post will henceforth be known as Fort Conger," Dolph announced.

The place was named after Congressman Edward Hurd Conger, who had originally introduced the bill to set up the expedition. The flag was handed to Sergeants Brainard and Israel, who climbed onto the roof and raised the banner to the top of the pole. The detachment saluted the Stars and Stripes snapping in the freezing wind.

After the ceremony Kislingbury came to Dolph. "The *Proteus* is getting up steam. My gear is packed and ready to take aboard her. I'd like my orders, if you please, Lieutenant Greely."

Dolph stared toward the ship, which was backing and filling, ramming its bow against the ice, trying to reach the open water which shimmered in the distance. He could see that the *Proteus* had a long struggle before she would break through.

The Last Outpost

"There's no hurry, Mr. Kislingbury," Dolph said. "Perhaps I still have time to change your mind."

"I do not want to serve under your command," Kislingbury said stiffly.

"Come into the house, then. I'll write out your orders," Dolph shrugged.

A few moments later he was at the field desk in the officers' room. As he dipped his pen into the inkwell, with Kislingbury watching, the whistle of the *Proteus* blared three times. Dolph rushed to the door. The *Proteus* had found a weak spot in the ice field and was slashing a path through to the open sea.

"I'm sorry, Mr. Kislingbury, but it would appear that you've lost your homebound passage," Dolph grinned. With his eyes twinkling he looked at the downcast officer. "Cheer up, Lieutenant. It's only your pride that was hurt. You'll have a full year in which to mend it—and in the months ahead I hope we'll be friends."

"Nothing in regulations states that I have to like you," Kislingbury retorted. "But I won't let my feelings interfere. I'll do my duty."

"That's good enough for me. You're dismissed," Dolph said.

Kislingbury saluted, did a smart about-face, and stepped outside. Everyone in camp stood silently staring after the ship which was vanishing toward the horizon, smoke pluming from her funnel. Dolph watched the ship until he could no longer see her even with binoculars. He went back into the house and closed the door. The *Proteus* had been the last link with civilization. Now she was gone. Dolph listened to the voices of the men talking outside. They would be looking to him for leadership and decisions. He could not make any mistakes. Outside, the rising wind wailed down on the camp from the unknown northern wastelands. Perhaps they would be able to uncover the secrets of the Arctic—or perhaps, as so many had before them, they might disappear in the frozen void.

The darkness of Arctic winter closed around them—a period when the sun came only briefly each day, and the rest of the time was spent in murky half-light. The men were kept busy; weather instruments had to be watched constantly, and hourly readings taken of atmospheric pressure, temperature, and dew point of the air. Every record was painstakingly written down.

The meteorologists noted the type and drift movement of the clouds. An accurate check of weather conditions was kept. The temperature of the water in the bay was registered both on the surface and, when possible, at extreme depths. The thickness of the ice at the shore line and farther out was frequently tested. Changes in the declination of the magnetic compass needle, due to their closeness to the North Pole, were precisely noted.

From time to time, samples of air were taken by filling and then tightly corking special bottles. This was done with a view to analyzing the specimens for oxygen content at various temperatures. Many of the observations made by this expedition were the first systematic ones ever carried out in the North.

After the daily routine had been established, Dolph placed Kislingbury in charge of Fort Conger and set out with Lieutenant Lockwood, Sergeant Brainard, Sergeant Israel, and Jens Edwards, the Eskimo hunter, to explore the western part of Grinnell Land, which had never been charted. A dog sled carried their supplies.

The group pushed in a westerly direction for several days. The landscape on every side was solidly frozen and piled high with snow. Even with snowshoes, progress was slow.

Jens Edwards ranged ahead, scouting the way. He traveled cautiously, for not even he had ever seen that part of Grinnell Land. After a five-day march Dolph decided to call off the westward expedition and return to Fort Conger. The terrain had become mountainous and nearly impassable. The explorers slipped on glacial ice, and the dogs could barely keep their footing on the slippery surface.

Dolph halted the men and they encamped to await Jens Edwards' return from a scouting trip. They huddled around a portable cookstove, trying to keep warm in the twenty-below-zero weather. Jens was gone a long time, but at last Sergeant Israel spied him coming across the ice field.

The Eskimo slid toward them, moving clumsily on his snowshoes. "Wonder what's chasing him?" Brainard asked. "He acts as though a pack of timber wolves was on his tail."

MAN AGAINST THE ELEMENTS

"Don't show your ignorance, Dave," Israel laughed. "There aren't any timber wolves this far north."

"Of course not," Brainard grumbled. "Wolves have too darned much sense to come here."

Jens Edwards stopped, raised his rifle, and fired three shots into the air. "Something's wrong. That's the distress signal!" Dolph cried. "Sergeant Israel, stay with the sled, Lockwood and Brainard, come with me!"

When they reached Jens, the Eskimo pointed excitedly to the west. "Lieutenant Greely! Quick! This way!"

"What is it, Jens?" Dolph asked.

"Wait! You see!"

They slogged on for half an hour and at last stood on the crest of a towering crag. "Down there," Jens said, gesturing. Dolph gasped at what he saw below. A valley, surrounded by the jutting, white-capped peaks of a mountain range, spread beneath. Through the mist that floated over the valley, Dolph saw a green forest without ice or snow.

He fumbled for his binoculars. A long ice-free lake stretched for miles. The woods were richly verdant. Due to some climatic freak, the temperature in that valley permitted the growth of foliage and trees in an atmosphere of eternal springtime.

I was down there, Lieutenant Greely," Jens said. "Much game in that forest. Musk ox. Caribou. Good hunting."

"Incredible," Dolph whispered. "A paradise in

this Arctic wilderness. A paradise, And we are the first outsiders to see it."

They climbed down the face of the crag and stood below, amidst the trees. A gentle breeze riffled the leaves. Brainard tore off his mittens and took the pad from his map case. He drew a map of the vicinity. After a while the men climbed back to the ice and snow above. On the crest they stared across the valley for a long time.

"Jens, I want you and Christiansen to lead a hunting party back here. The boys in camp will enjoy fresh meat," Dolph said.

"Me and Christiansen. We get plenty musk ox. Good hunting," Jens nodded.

Before leaving they named the lake Hazen Lake after General Hazen. They called the mountains that surrounded the valley the United States Range. Then they struggled back to where Sergeant Israel was anxiously waiting.

"I'd given up on you," Israel complained to Brainard. "What kept you so long? And what was it Jens found out there?"

"He found the Garden of Eden," Brainard said.

"Come on, Dave—I'm in no mood for fooling. What was it he found?"

"I told you. The Garden of Eden! Now let's not waste any more time gabbing, Ed. Lieutenant Greely wants us to start for the base camp right away."

Israel opened his mouth to say something, thought better of it, and waved his hand in disgust. "The Garden of Eden, my foot!" he muttered, stumbling off in the snow to hitch up the dogs.

· · · CHAPTER 12

The Brink of Eternity

THE LONG WINTER OF 1881–82 PASSED without discomfort for the men in Fort Conger. The Eskimo hunters brought in a steady supply of fresh meat from the green valley. Everyone in the expedition kept healthy and fully occupied.

Dolph was well pleased with the way things were running. Even Lieutenant Kislingbury seemed to have forgotten his grudge and at times was cordial toward Dolph. However, in December, 1881, a minor disorder erupted among the enlisted men. The troublemaker was Private Charles Henry, a volunteer from the Fifth Cavalry. Henry had sailed the Arctic before as a crew member on a whaling ship. He was a surly, powerfully built man described by Brainard as "going around with a chip on his shoulder."

Henry was on detail in the kitchen, where he provoked a fight with Private Julius Fredericks, the cook. The men were slugging it out when Dolph and Lieutenant Lockwood broke up the brawl.

"If there is any repetition of this, I'll court-martial the man responsible," Dolph warned. "I'll tolerate no disorder in my command. Is that understood?"

Both soldiers nodded. "Go on back to work," Dolph told them.

"I don't trust Henry," Lockwood observed. "There's something about the man—"

"Oh, he's quick-tempered, that's all. In the spring, when the sun returns and the ice breaks up, he'll be all right," Dolph reassured him. "You can't really blame anyone for losing his head in this cold and gloom."

"I suppose not, sir. We've all been working hard."

"Very hard." Dolph adjusted his eyeglasses. "Do you know the date, Mr. Lockwood?"

"December twenty-third, I believe, sir!"

"Yes. Two days before Christmas."

"Christmas!" Lockwood cried. "I hadn't thought of it!"

"I think we should celebrate with a party," Dolph said. "Jens came in with a good supply of meat yesterday. I'll have the cooks prepare a special dinner."

The Christmas meal served at Fort Conger was practically a feast. The menu included roast caribou, musk-ox tenderloin, plum pudding, dates, figs, nuts, candies, coffee, chocolates, hot rum, and cigars.

But the high point came while the men, filled with good food, were contentedly puffing on their cigars. Dolph stepped out of the house and returned a few minutes later carrying a full duffel bag. He took from it a handsomely wrapped package for each man. He had thought of the gifts before the expedition sailed.

The gesture was typical of Dolph. In his diary Sergeant Brainard characterized him in this way: "He was a silent, often taciturn man, but his tender heart and unfailing fairness won him the affection and loyalty of his command under difficult circumstances."

It was at the Christmas party that his rift with Lieutenant Kislingbury was finally ended. After the presents had been distributed Kislingbury rose, holding the pipe Dolph had given him.

"Lieutenant Greely, you should have ordered me bucked and gagged instead of handing me this gift. I've been a darned fool these past months and I want to publicly apologize for my conduct."

"Forget it, Mr. Kislingbury," Dolph laughed.

"I'm lucky the *Proteus* left before I could get on board," Kislingbury said. He lifted his mug of rum. "Gentlemen, I propose a toast." Everyone scraped to his feet. "Lieutenant Greely! Our gallant commander!" Kislingbury cried.

The tin mugs clanked across the table. "Lieutenant Greely!" all repeated.

Later Sergeant Israel played his harmonica. Private Maurice Connell, who was only twenty, the youngest in the detachment, gave a concert on an accordion.

There was group singing and the men's voices blended in many favorite old ballads: "Home Sweet Home," "Tenting Tonight," "Lorena," and a dozen others. They harmonized Christmas carols such as "O Little Town of Bethlehem," "Silent Night, Holy Night," "Adeste Fideles," "God Rest Ye Merry Gentlemen," and as many more as they could remember.

Tears filled their eyes and the memories of home brought nostalgic thoughts. Dolph thought tenderly of Henrietta and his little girls. Outside, the howling wind suddenly died down and in the stillness the singing carried far out into the silent, frozen wasteland.

The winter dragged on until the first week of March, 1882, when the sun burst out to explode the wintry gloom. It came in a flash of bright yellow. Although everyone had been awaiting the sun, its sudden appearance was a surprise. The men cheered, thumped one other, and wrestled in the snow. Their spirits soared and everyone worked with fresh energy. The sunlight brought new beauty— and the snow-covered icecap sparkled merrily.

At the end of March the weather turned favorable enough for them to attempt a long-range exploration. Dolph planned to take a party north from Lady Franklin Bay along the coast of Grinnell Land, then across the ice in Robeson Channel to the northernmost tip of Greenland. The explorers proposed to reach the North Pole if that were possible.

However, while on a routine inspection, Dolph suffered a leg injury and was forced to limp around on a cane. Obviously he could not make the trip. He sent for Kislingbury and Lockwood, spread out a map, and outlined to them the route he had hoped to follow.

"Which one of you wants to take this mission?" he asked.

"I do!" they cried together.

"I can spare only one officer," Dolph said. "We'll let the cards decide who is to go." He opened a drawer and took out a pack of playing cards. "One cut apiece, gentlemen. High card goes."

Kislingbury turned up the jack of spades.

Lockwood, the king of hearts. "Mr. Lockwood, you're the man. I envy you," Dolph said.

"And so do I," Kislingbury added.

At daybreak, April 3, 1882, Lieutenant Lockwood left camp with Sergeant Brainard and Privates Connell, Long, and Whisler. A sled drawn by the strongest huskies in the dog pack carried scientific apparatus. Just before they pushed off, Dolph had a parting word with Lockwood.

"You will go as far north as possible without endangering either your men or yourself. My hope is that you will reach the pole—it remains, however, only a hope. Do the best you can."

"Count on that, sir," Lockwood said.

"You may leave at once, Mr. Lockwood. Good luck." Dolph shook his hand.

The whole detachment turned out to see the party leave. This was the most ambitious exploration the Greely Expedition had yet attempted.

Lockwood signaled to Brainard, who cracked a bull whip over the dogs. "Mush!" he shouted.

A cheer rose from the onlookers, and soon Lock-

The Brink of Eternity

wood was out of sight. Fort Conger returned to its daily details. As the days stretched out, Dolph started to worry about the explorers. The party had taken along rations to last sixty days, but the weather had unexpectedly turned foul: a succession of sleet, rain, fog, and high winds. Dolph knew the bad weather would throw Lockwood off schedule and possibly force him to stay out after his food supply was exhausted.

On June 10, the fifty-ninth day of Lockwood's absence, Dolph, whose leg had now healed, decided to lead a search for the party. His sleds were already being loaded when Corporal Joe Elison, the duty noncom at the weather station, rushed to him.

"Lieutenant! Lieutenant! They're here!" Elison panted.

Lockwood and his men staggered into camp behind their sled. The dogs pulling it could barely stand. The men were ragged and exhausted. Dolph hurried to them.

"Lieutenant Lockwood and party reporting, sir," the weary officer croaked, managing a salute. Brainard and the three privates straightened up at Dolph's approach.

"At ease, lads. At ease. This is no time for military formality. You need hot food and rest. Report to me when you feel up to it," Dolph said.

That evening Lockwood gave his account of the trip. "We had a bad time almost from the outset. The weather was awful. I feared we would use up our rations. Fortunately Private Long shot a seal and we had enough food." He walked to the map on the wall and pointed. "On May 13 we reached here—eighty-three degrees, twenty-four minutes, north latitude. forty degrees, forty minutes, west longitude."

Dolph clapped him on the shoulder. "Lockwood! You came closer to the North Pole than anyone in history! That calls for a drink!"

He filled two glasses with brandy. As they sipped the liquor, he asked, "What is it like at the top of the world, Mr. Lockwood?"

"It's hard to put into words, sir." Lockwood's brow furrowed. "You feel alone—lost—surrounded by the glacier; and the only sound is the wind, cracking like artillery in the cold. You look across the emptiness and you think this was how it must have been in the beginning of the world." Lockwood stared into his brandy glass. "I'm just a plain man, sir. Talking doesn't come easy to me." He glanced up and met Dolph's eyes. "But I'll tell you how it is up there, Lieutenant. You're standing on the brink of eternity, afraid you'll fall over the edge. That's what it's like, sir."

· · · CHAPTER 13

The Retreat

A CARNIVAL-LIKE SPIRIT SPREAD THROUGH Fort Conger in the summer of 1882 as the time for the arrival of the relief ship drew closer. Dolph spent many hours each day atop a hill that overlooked Lady Franklin Bay, scanning the horizon for the ship. All through July he kept up his daily vigil.

He would not admit even to Lockwood and Kislingbury that he had begun to feel some doubt about the vessel's arrival. None of his misgivings was apparent to the men. Bets were being made as to the exact date and hour the relief ship would be sighted. Even Doctor Pavy, the sour-faced surgeon, managed to squeeze out a smile now and then.

But with the approach of August the first signs of winter came. On August 1 there were snow flurries. Drift ice formed in the bay and the temperature began a swift decline until the numbing cold brought thick floes to choke the open water. By August 15 Dolph was convinced that something had gone wrong with the relief vessel. He called a conference with his officers and noncoms.

"I think we must accept the fact that no ship will be here this summer," Dolph told them. "Keep close tabs on your men. Report any breach of discipline to me. We may have to face a serious morale problem when the men realize no relief is at hand."

"The ship may yet turn up, sir," Kislingbury said.

"That's not very probable. Winter is only weeks away. I believe that the relief ship ran into foul weather in Smith Sound—ice, storms, or even worse. But, according to the plan, the relief ship was to leave notice at Capes Hawks, Isabella, and Sabine—and also to set up supply depots wherever possible. I'll send search parties out to scour those areas."

On August 19, 1882, Lieutenant Kislingbury left Camp Conger to look for the supply dumps. He led a five-man team along the east coast of Grinnell Land. After marching south for three days, the search group was hit by a blizzard. An avalanche buried their dog sled, and the men barely managed to make it back to Fort Conger.

Then the weather worsened. Snow, rain, fog, and wind brought with them the fiercest cold the men had yet faced during their year in the Arctic. On some days the temperature reached seventy to eighty degrees below zero. Under such conditions only the most essential work could be done. The men idled the hours in the house playing chess and checkers, reading, and gambling. One marathon poker game went on for seventy-two hours without letup.

The Retreat

The long night of winter set in and the men grew morose and sullen. Discontented mutterings were heard for the first time.

Brainard wrote in his diary:

> This is a trying period. No relief ship. No mail from home. We have suffered a cruel blow. Only such a setback could have broken our spirits. Before, we had hope. Now our position is plain. We are cut off from the world at least until next year, which seems an eternity away.

Fortunately no food shortage threatened them. Just before the foul weather set in, Jens and Christiansen had made a hunting trip to the valley with Private Long. They had bagged a huge amount of game. Whole sides of musk-ox and caribou meat, dressed and trimmed, hung in the cold-storage bin. According to Long, "We brought in enough meat to have fed the Army of the Potomac for a month."

No day passed that winter without snow or sleet, fog or freezing rain. The men finally accepted the fact that no ship would come until the following summer. Once they had made that adjustment, morale rose again. Despite the fierce weather all stations were manned, observations taken, and specimens collected. In January the temperatures eased a bit, and soon there were signs that the bitter winter was ending. The days grew brighter and weak sunlight pierced the darkness for a few hours, at least.

Waning winter stirred talk about the 1883 relief ship and, while his hopes were strong, Dolph had to prepare for any eventuality. He conferred with Lockwood and Kislingbury. "We must draw up plans now for a possible retreat to Cape Sabine, if the ship does not come in August," he announced.

"It will be here, sir," Kislingbury said.

"I think so, too," Dolph agreed. "But we must get ready for the worst."

The three officers drew up an evacuation plan. If no ship dropped anchor in Lady Franklin Bay by August 8, 1883, the detachment would abandon Fort Conger on the ninth. The move was to be made in the steam launch, *Lady Greely,* and the lifeboats. The bulk of the rations and equipment would be distributed among the three lifeboats, while the scientific data collected at Fort Conger would be taken in the launch. Most members of the party were to be carried in the lifeboats with the launch towing them.

According to the plan the expedition would head into Smith Sound, where the relief ship might be awaiting their arrival. In the event that no ship was there, a sharp lookout was to be kept for the detachment which the relief ship should have left behind with supplies and mail. If no contact at all was made, Dolph was then to lead his men to Cape Sabine for a rendezvous with a third relief ship in 1884.

Having drawn his withdrawal plans, Dolph once again took an exploration team into western Grinnell Land. There he charted the entire region

The Retreat

around Hazen Lake—the first time it had ever been mapped. In the United States Mountain Range he discovered five giant glaciers, each with a front a mile wide and one hundred and sixty-five feet high—up to then, they were the largest glaciers ever found in the Arctic.

At the same time, Lockwood was surveying the territory to the northeast, making the pioneer maps of the unknown territory known as Grant Land. In this way they passed the spring. At last the ice broke up in the channels, and the way was clear for a ship to sail in from the south.

Once again the men scanned the waters for a sign of the relief ship. They waited and watched—but none came. The summer was a brief one in 1883. By mid-June there were snow flurries and harsh winds ruffling Smith Sound. As July slipped past, gloom settled over Fort Conger. Now the men were openly saying they had been forsaken by their leaders in Washington.

On August 1 Dolph ordered the steam launch and the lifeboats to be loaded and preparations for evacuation started. Every piece of scientific apparatus was carefully dismantled and wrapped in oilcloth for its protection. The specimen jars were stored in lined containers and shielded against breakage. All journals, notebooks, diaries, records, maps, and charts were sewed into canvas sacks and then wrapped up in waterproofed cloth bags. The boxes of records and scientific equipment went with Dolph on the *Lady Greely*.

"I'd rather lose my life than this material," he told Lockwood.

The night of August 7–8, 1883, no one in Fort Conger slept. Every man in the party stood at the water's edge, peering into the darkness, praying to see a ship's light bobbing in the harbor. They saw only Arctic blackness.

"Gentlemen, we will move tomorrow at daybreak according to plan," Dolph announced at a meeting of the whole force. "Only the arrival of the relief ship will cancel that order."

August 9 dawned bleak and foggy. The launch swayed at anchor, steam up in its boiler. The lifeboats, tied together in a row, were fastened to the launch. Each of the smaller craft carried boxes of provisions—enough, it had been figured, to last until the summer of 1884. The men boarded the boats. Lockwood took charge of the first lifeboat; Kislingbury commanded the last one in line.

Soon everyone except Dolph and Jens Edwards had embarked. The Eskimo walked back into the camp. He went into the kennel where the huskies were penned. The animals came running to him, barking. Jens unslung his rifle. He shot the dogs, one after another.

There were tears in his eyes when he came back to Dolph. "We go now," Jens said.

Dolph placed his hand gently on the hunter's shoulder. "You know it had to be done, Jens. We could not let them run loose up here with winter coming."

The Retreat

"Better for them to die at the hands of a friend," Jens said.

They stepped into the launch. Dolph signaled Sergeant William H. Cross, who was at the wheel of the *Lady Greely*. The launch's steam whistle tooted. Her propeller churned. She moved slowly out with the three lifeboats strung behind. No one spoke. Only the steady throbbing of the launch's engine and her thrashing propeller disturbed the stillness.

Dolph looked back at Fort Conger with a touch of sadness. The flag still waved boldly from the top of the house. He had done his duty and obeyed his orders. If the expedition was destined now to end in failure, it was not his fault or his men's. They had carried out everything that had been asked of them. Dolph knew that, no matter what might happen now, the Lady Franklin Bay Expedition had achieved much. It had recorded precise meteorological data and made new maps of Greenland's northern coastline—maps proving almost conclusively that it was an island.

But even beyond the scientific and cartographic value of the expedition, Dolph had demonstrated that a party properly equipped and supplied could stay safely in the Arctic for two years.

If only they had not left us in the lurch, he thought. If only those relief ships had come through to us. It was too late for regrets. The main problem now was to accomplish the retreat successfully.

· · · CHAPTER 14

The Ordeal Begins

ALMOST FROM THE START THE RETREAT RAN into trouble. The boats had been out less than a day when a gale whipped through Smith Sound. Sergeant Cross was barely able to run the launch into a cove without capsizing. The last boat in line shipped water and, although Kislingbury and his crew bailed desperately, the boat kept settling until they were forced to abandon it. The men transferred into the other two boats and the launch, but the supplies could not be saved and they went down to the bottom with the boat. Valuable food and clothing were lost in that mishap.

The party sat out the blow in the cove. Waves splashed over the boats, coating them with glaze ice. All were drenched, and their garments froze solid. They could do nothing but wait in discomfort until the wind died down and the Sound became navigable once more.

After several hours Dolph's flotilla was able to move southward again. Everyone hoped to see the relief ship around the next bend. But after several days of slow progress that hope diminished. Bitter weather set in and huge cakes of ice drifted in Smith Sound. Two giant floes pinched and crushed the remaining lifeboats. Fortunately the men were able to salvage the supplies and get them safely aboard the launch, but that sturdy vessel could not carry so much cargo.

Reluctantly Dolph ordered the *Lady Greely* unloaded and abandoned to the icy sound. The rations, supplies, and scientific equipment were lashed to sleds and, when that work was finished, Dolph addressed his men as they stood together upon an ice floe that stretched solidly for miles.

"Lads, we're going on to Cape Sabine. There we'll set up camp until this coming August, when the rescue ship will arrive to take us home," he said, shouting to make himself heard above the wind that shrieked across the icecap.

"Don't try to make it easy, Lieutenant! We're never getting out of this God-forsaken place alive," a soldier cried.

"That's not so," Dolph snapped. "Let's hear no more such talk. Remember, lads, to die is easy, very easy—it's only hard to strive, to endure, to live! Now let's move out. Everyone will take turns hauling the sleds—officers and noncommissioned officers as well." He pointed to the south. "Yonder lies Cape Sabine. Keep up your courage and we'll get there!"

Weighted down by cumbersome packs, the party struggled on slowly. Hand-hauling the sleds was difficult and exhausting. The cases of scientific specimens and instruments were particularly heavy.

Dolph told the men pulling a sled laden with a tankful of marine specimens, "The task will be easier if you'd get rid of that."

"No, sir," a soldier spat, "we ain't tossing away two years of work."

The awful trek seemed endless. They had never felt such cold. It was impossible to pitch a proper camp. Tents were blown away by the wind. So the men slept on the ground in their sleeping bags. At first Dolph tried to have at least one hot meal a day served to his men, but this could not be done. They ate as they could, and a meal was often only a few strips of dried caribou meat.

This continued day after day—with nothing to show but a few painfully gained miles on the road to Cape Sabine. The men grew weaker, and they covered shorter distances every day.

On September 29, 1883, fifty-one days after leaving Fort Conger, the exhausted men stumbled into the huts that had been erected by a previous expedition at a place called Eskimo Point, some twenty miles north of Cape Sabine. The weather was bad; the wind whipped a fine snow into swirling clouds. Dolph saw that his men could go no farther. He called a halt in the abandoned camp. The huts were still habitable, although unused for many years, and for the first time in nearly two months the men slept under a roof.

In a few days they turned the camp into winter quarters. The largest hut was set aside as the bunkhouse. Each night the men simply unrolled their sleeping bags on the floor. In the morning the bags were rolled up and the room became the expedition's headquarters.

A second hut housed the precious records and scientific data they had gathered at Lady Franklin Bay. The third, with Sergeant Brainard in charge, was both cook-shack and supply room. Everyone except Brainard was forbidden to enter the shack without permission from Dolph.

The provisions were stored in the supply hut. Brainard checked the cases of canned food, the boxes of hardtack, the frozen meat and dehydrated vegetables. He made a frightening discovery.

"There is on hand only enough food for forty days at full rations," he reported to Dolph.

"But we carried along enough from Fort Conger to last until next summer." Dolph buried his face in his hands for a moment and then looked up. "I tried to think of everything, Brainard. I could not foresee that all three lifeboats would sink and take our food under the ice in Smith Sound."

"We're in a bad spot, sir," Brainard said.

"If we could only find the supplies the relief ships must have left for us at Cape Sabine—" Dolph slammed a fist into his palm. "If we could only find them—"

"With your permission, sir, I'll try to reach Cape Sabine," Brainard offered.

"You can't go out in that blizzard, Sergeant. But when the weather clears, you may make a try. I'll send the Eskimo hunters and Private Long to look for game in the area. Now we have to wait for better weather," Dolph said.

The weather eased on October 10. Jens Edwards, Christiansen, and Long took off to search for musk ox, caribou, or seal. Lieutenant Lockwood and Sergeant Brainard led a detail to search for the supply cache at Cape Sabine.

A week later the hunters returned. Long was carrying Christiansen on his back and Jens Edwards could barely hobble. Both Eskimos had suffered severe frostbite on their hands and feet. Rugged Francis Long was unaffected by the rigors of the trip.

After turning the Eskimos over to Doctor Pavy, Long reported to Dolph. "We roved thirty miles, sir. There's no living creature anywhere about. Nothing grows here and nothing lives."

The Lockwood–Brainard detachment returned three days later with two injured men—Private Jacob Bender, his leg broken in a fall, and Corporal Joe Elison, with frostbitten hands and feet. Once again Doctor Pavy was busy treating casualties.

Lockwood and Brainard stumbled into the main house, where Dolph was waiting for them.

"Did you have any luck, Lockwood?" Dolph asked eagerly.

"Yes, sir. We reached Cape Sabine and found that last year's supply ship had left supplies for us—"

"Oh, that's fine! Good work, good work!" Dolph cried.

"The ship was called the *Neptune*, sir." Lockwood continued. "We found this." He handed an

The Ordeal Begins

oilskin pouch to Dolph. It contained a letter, which Dolph read quickly.

"I see. The *Neptune* couldn't get through Smith Sound because of ice, so she left her supplies at Cape Sabine," Dolph said, looking up. "But we're all right now. How many men will you need to haul in the supplies, Mr. Lockwood?"

"Not many, sir," Brainard cut in bitterly. He turned to Lockwood. "Tell him about the supplies, Lieutenant. Tell him."

Lockwood took a deep breath. "Yes, the *Neptune* left supplies—cases of food, clothing, sacks of mail. But that relief party must have been in an all-fired hurry to get away from there. They left everything in the open, unprotected. and it's almost all spoiled, ruined—the meat, the hardtack, the tinned food— the cans rusted through." Lockwood choked back an angry sob.

"I don't—I don't understand," Dolph said. "All they had to do was cover the cases with tarpaulin to protect them from the weather . . ." He paused and sighed. "But we can't undo what's been done. Is it possible to salvage anything, Mr. Lockwood?"

"I guess so, sir. We didn't examine everything thoroughly. Bender broke his leg, and poor Elison got frostbite. He was digging in a snowdrift to reach what he thought were boxes of food. He worked for hours only to turn up a dozen mailsacks. The letters had been soaked into pulp. Well, his hands were in bad shape. So I decided to bring the injured men back as quickly as I could."

"That was sound judgment, Mr. Lockwood. Sergeant Brainard, draw a map showing the exact location of the supplies. Mr. Kislingbury will take a detail there and bring out what he can salvage."

Even with the dozen cases of tinned food Kislingbury brought out of the supply dump, the food situation grew desperate. All supplies were depleted—especially medical stores. Daily hunting parties went out but never made a kill. Dolph had to put the men on half rations in November. Everyone lost weight. The only way to save strength was by resting almost all day, and the men stayed in their sleeping bags most of the time.

On December 1 the temperature once again dropped suddenly to eighty degrees below zero. The day before Christmas—a cheerless one compared to their first Yuletide in the Arctic—Doctor Pavy, the humorless surgeon, stepped out of the hut and walked off into the darkness. No one ever saw him again. A note was found pinned to his sleeping bag:

TO ALL MY GALLANT FRIENDS:

I am leaving you. This will mean one less to feed. I am leaving because this is the only way I can now help you. A doctor is only a mere man. Without medicines, I am useless to you —and the medical supplies are gone. You must all be brave and trust in God. In His mercy, He will deliver you.

OCTAVE PAVY, M.D.
Surgeon, U.S. Army

The Ordeal Begins

On New Year's Day, Private Jacob Bender died quietly in his sleep. He was in constant pain from his broken leg—weakened by the lack of food, he simply passed away. His companions buried him, scraping out a shallow grave in the snow. Dolph read the burial service.

The men grew moody, crushed by despair. They were listless and dispirited. Still, Dolph managed to keep some activity going. Every night he held what became known as "Greely's Hour." During the period he delivered lectures on various subjects. He talked about every state in the Union, told Civil War stories, recalled his frontier days, and read to the men. He encouraged others to join in the discussion. It was this diversion alone that kept the survivors sane.

One night, after "Greely's Hour," Sergeant Brainard came into the hut. He went to Dolph, who was lying in his sleeping bag.

"I must have a word with you, sir," Brainard whispered urgently.

"Yes, Sergeant?"

"I have bad news, sir. Someone is stealing food from the supply room. A slab of bacon is gone."

Dolph sat up and gazed about the room. One of the men lying there was guilty.

"We must find the thief, Brainard. We must find him," he said softly.

· · · CHAPTER 15

The Ordeal Ends

DOLPH INFORMED LOCKWOOD AND KISlingbury about what had happened. The two officers and Brainard set up a guard on the supply shack. Brainard rigged a booby trap triggered by a trip rope. Anyone entering the shack, unaware of the rope, would catch his foot in it, bringing down on him a pile of empty cracker boxes. He would be pinned under the crates long enough to be captured.

In the early hours of January 9, 1884, a terrific crash came from the supply room. Lockwood and Kislingbury were out the door in a moment, followed by Dolph. The officers ran to the shack. There they found Brainard, his pistol leveled, covering a man struggling to get out from beneath the crates.

"Keep your hands up and come out where we can see you," Brainard ordered.

The thief emerged. He was Private Charles Henry. "I ain't done anything," he said. "I was only getting wood for the fire."

The Ordeal Ends

"Bring him into the hut and search him. I want all the men to see this," Dolph said.

Brainard pushed Henry into the shack. Everyone was awake, blinking in the lamplight.

"What's the matter? What's he done?" a soldier asked.

"I accuse this man of stealing food for himself. Search him, Sergeant Brainard," Dolph commanded.

Brainard found three cans of tomatoes and a package of hardtack hidden under Henry's coat. A growl went up from the men.

"You thieving dog!" Julius Fredericks cried, lunging at Henry.

Dolph grabbed the angry man. "None of that! He'll be tried as a soldier. I'll have no mob violence here! Remember, this is a military unit!" he cried sharply.

"Military unit!" Henry spat. "Military unit! That's a laugh! Listen! He calls us soldiers. Sure, we're soldiers, left up here until the last man is dead! And for what? We've been bilked, boys! And now we're trapped. Sure I stole food. At least I'll die with a full belly!"

"That's enough, Henry!" Dolph snapped. "Mr. Lockwood, detail a guard over the prisoner. All noncoms and officers meet me in ten minutes. We are holding a court-martial in the supply room."

The court sentenced Private Charles Henry to death before a firing squad at the discretion of the commanding officer. Dolph went off by himself to ponder his decision. If he spared the thief, others would be encouraged to steal the little food that was left. His main concern was the survival of all and not the fate of one man. He remembered Colonel Fischer tapping his insignia and saying, "This eagle can be a bird of prey."

Dolph approved the verdict. The next morning the men drew lots to make up the firing squad. Four pieces of paper were marked with an *X;* the rest were blank. Those who drew the *X*'s comprised the squad. Kislingbury commanded the detail. They marched Henry a few hundred yards from camp and carried out the sentence.

His last words were "Go ahead and shoot. You'll all be joining me soon enough."

The cold weather ended unexpectedly. There was sunshine in February and the weakened, emaciated men crawled out of the house to blink stupidly in the sunlight. The mere sight of it gave them renewed hope.

Jens Edwards and Christiansen had recovered from their frostbite. They ventured on a hunting trip with Long. The ice was breaking up in Smith Sound. Jens spied a small seal resting on a slowly drifting floe, almost four hundred yards offshore.

"Look there, Long!" he cried.

Francis Long raised his rifle. The Eskimos dropped to their knees, watching him—their lips moving in prayer. He took deliberate aim. His shot was true.

"Got him!" he exulted. "But how in blazes are we going to bring him in?"

"Me and Christiansen, we go out on the floe.

The Ordeal Ends

Cut up seal. Bring him to shore a few pieces at a time. You go back to camp. Get sled. Men to pull it."

Long hurried to the huts. Dolph hugged the soldier when he heard the news. The men cheered and pounded one another on the back.

"Don't waste your strength that way," Dolph warned. "I want a dozen men to pull the sled."

In minutes, volunteers had grabbed the drag ropes of a sled. They hauled it out of camp behind Long.

The starving soldiers dined on roasted seal meat that night, but they ate joylessly. Jens Edwards had slipped off the ice floe while carrying the last chunk of meat to shore. Weighted down by his cumbersome clothing, he had drowned. In a vain effort to save his friend, Christiansen leaped in after him. When Long arrived with the sled the Eskimo was lying on shore, half-frozen. He gasped out his story before he, too, died.

The unseasonably warm weather continued, but that seal was the last game either Long or anyone else could find. On February 22, 1884, Dolph decided there might be a chance to find help in Greenland, across the sound.

"We're not too distant from the Etah Eskimos. A hunting party might spot us—or we might be able to hunt some food," he told his officers. "We must make a move—staying here, like this, is certain death."

"If the ice is solid, we can do it," Lockwood said.

Brainard divided the rations, setting aside an

equal portion for each man. "There is a quarter of a pound of meat and a half pound of hardtack daily—enough food to last until April tenth," he reported.

The twenty men still left of the original twenty-five waited for a cold snap. It came on March 1. Smith Sound froze again. On that date the men stumbled away from camp. They carried their packs and rifles and hauled on sleds the data they had collected. A solid ice field stretched into the sound, but ended five hundred yards from Greenland. Clear water lapped at the edges of the pack. With no way to cross over they returned to the camp.

Two more men died before the end of March. In April, Kislingbury collapsed from malnutrition. He clutched Dolph's hand as he lay dying.

"I'm proud to have served with you, sir," he whispered.

Dolph turned away, weeping. He felt betrayed. They had all been betrayed. He thought of Henrietta and his daughters. He would never see the girls grown up. All they would know about him was that he had died in a faraway place—and all they would have left of their father was a faded photograph. He regretted that he would forever be a stranger to his children.

Men died one after another, with neither prayers nor tears. Lockwood lived until May 1 and his death left alive only Dolph, Brainard, Elison, Long, Fredericks, Connell, and Biederbeck.

The food supply dwindled. By June 19 just three

The Ordeal Ends

days' rations remained. When that was gone, there would be nothing. Earlier the survivors had chosen to stay outdoors in the sunlight and the mild weather. They felt it was easier to die under the open sky.

While they still had strength, Fredericks and Biederbeck had constructed a shelter of sorts from empty ration boxes. They also rigged a tent for Dolph, setting it a little apart. He was no longer able to stand, but rested all day in a sitting position.

Brainard and Long stubbornly refused to give up. Each morning they crawled to the top of a ridge that overlooked the water, watching for the rescue ship or even an Eskimo kayak carrying a lone seal hunter—someone, anyone, another human being to help them. Elison, Connell, Biederbeck, and Fredericks were resigned to death. They seldom moved from their sleeping bags. So they waited —seven men in an alien land. Seven hopeless men. . . .

But while the survivors at Eskimo Point were waiting to die, they could not know that back in the United States many thousands of everyday Americans were determined to do something for them.

The first two relief ships had failed to reach the men at Lady Franklin Bay—the *Neptune* dropping its supplies and turning tail in 1882. In 1883 two ships, the *Proteus* and the *Yantic,* had been sent but ran into bad luck. The *Proteus* was pinched in the ice at Smith Sound and went down with the bulk of the supplies for the Greely Expedition.

As a result of these two failures, Secretary of War Robert T. Lincoln announced that in the opinion of many experts "no party could sustain itself for two years in the Arctic without receiving supplies. Undoubtedly the gallant men of Lady Franklin Bay are dead. It is doubtful that any further attempts will be made to reach them."

This statement raised a storm throughout the United States. Letters by the thousands poured in on Congress demanding the dispatch of a third rescue force. Shipowners offered their vessels for the effort, and a group of wealthy New Yorkers raised funds to outfit a private rescue party. Several Chicago businessmen put up a twenty-five-thousand-dollar reward for the rescue of Greely. Newspapers ran articles urging that Greely be saved, or at least that the fate of the expedition be definitely determined.

Among those who fought on to raise a relief force was Henrietta Greely. No thought of surrender ever entered her mind. She left the children with her parents in San Diego, moved to Washington, and dedicated all her time and energy to Dolph's cause. She haunted the offices of Representatives and Senators, goading them into action. The slim, beautiful woman soon became a familiar figure on Capitol Hill. Wherever she turned, Henrietta aroused sympathy on every side.

In April, President Chester Alan Arthur, who

The Ordeal Ends

had succeeded to the office in 1881 after President James Garfield's assassination, finally intervened.

"We cannot, in honor, merely abandon those courageous Americans who endangered their lives in that distant Arctic outpost," he said. "If they still live, we must bring them home. If they have died in the line of duty, it is incumbent upon us to bury them in a manner befitting heroes of the nation."

He decided that, since the army had twice failed, this rescue mission would be under naval command. The President called in Secretary of the Navy William Eaton Chandler.

"You will organize a suitably equipped force under competent command. I charge you with impressing those who undertake this duty that no hazards must deter them," he ordered. "The nation, the whole world expects this mission to succeed. Our prayers, hopes, and national prestige sail with your ships."

Chandler selected one of the navy's ablest officers, Captain Winfield Scott Schley, to lead the rescue. Schley assembled a fleet of three ships—the *Thetis,* the *Bear,* and the *Alert.* The *Thetis,* flagship of the flotilla, was under his command. For skipper of the *Bear,* he chose Lieutenant William Emory, a tough regular who had sailed in the Arctic. The master of the *Alert* was Captain G. W. Coffin, a Civil War combat veteran.

The fleet steamed out of St. John's, Newfoundland, on May 22, 1884. Prior to sailing, Schley addressed the assembled ships' companies—all navy volunteers.

"We are going to find Greely dead or alive. We will not flinch or shirk. This is a battle in a war. The Arctic is our enemy. The lives of brave men may depend on you. Do not fail them!"

The thaw had come early that year. The three ships brushed aside the floating ice and slashed a passage into Smith Sound, with the *Thetis* in the lead.

The squadron reached Cape Sabine on June 22, 1884, and, finding no one there, pushed on farther north. Lieutenant Emory, standing watch on the bridge of the *Bear*, swept the barren hummocks with his powerful binoculars as the ships headed past Eskimo Point. At that moment Brainard and Long dragged themselves to the top of the ridge.

They saw the ships at the same time. "My God, Long!" Brainard murmured. "My God, they've come!"

Helping each other stand, they waved frantically. Emory spotted them. He turned to the signalman on duty. "I've found Greely! Signal Captain Schley."

A longboat was swiftly lowered and in a little while the landing party was scrambling up to Long and Brainard, who were sitting in the snow, clinging to each other and sobbing.

"Are there any others?" Emory asked.

"Down there." Long pointed.

The ships launched more boats. Stretcher bearers and doctors came ashore. Brainard and Long

The Ordeal Ends

were tenderly carried to a boat and rowed out to the *Alert*.

Captain Schley landed and joined Emory. Captain Coffin brought a detail—and sailors swarmed over the ridge, hurrying to the camp.

"Where is Lieutenant Greely?" Schley called out.

"I am Greely," Dolph gasped.

Schley later wrote:

> At the moment of rescue, Greely was unable to stand alone and was almost helpless. His appearance was wild; his hair long and matted, his face and hands covered with dirt; his form wasted almost to a skeleton; his feet and hands swollen, his eyes sunken, and his body covered with filthy and almost worn-out garments that had not been changed for six or eight months.

The survivors were carried off on litters, but Dolph refused to let them move him until he saw the records and research material on the way to the ships.

"Greely, every moment counts for you," Schley said. "It is vital that you have medical attention. Are those papers and specimens worth the risk of your life?"

"Yes, Captain," Dolph smiled wanly. "Eighteen of my men died to gather those data. I can surely spare a few minutes to be sure they are safe."

"You're a stubborn man, Lieutenant," Schley said, patting him on the shoulder.

"I am, Captain—otherwise I would be dead, too," Dolph said.

After a week of proper care and food aboard the *Thetis*, Dolph was strong enough to sit on deck in the sunshine. The ships were cruising south. The air was sharp. He leaned back in his chair and squinted at the clean sky. It was sweet to be alive.

He was going home to Henrietta. And his daughters would not grow up without their father. He sighed with content, closed his eyes, and slept. The ordeal was ended.

• • • CHAPTER 16

Through the Years

MULTICOLORED FLAGS FLUTTERED IN THE sunlight from the rigging of the United States warships riding at anchor off Portsmouth, New Hampshire, on Friday, August 8, 1884. Almost the whole Atlantic fleet—cruisers, gunboats, and battleships—was gathered in the harbor. The ships had been newly painted for this occasion. The white hulls were spotless. The deck brass gleamed. Even the gun barrels had been polished to mirror brightness.

The ships' companies, wearing starched white summer uniforms, were arrayed in parade formation. Aboard the squadron flagship, the battlewagon U.S.S. *Tennessee,* a band played on the forward gun deck. The brassy music carried to the thousands of people massed along the shore line, on the breakwater and the quay.

The small garrisons of Fort Constitution, on Seavey's Island, and Fort Point, on Kittrey's Island, stood to cannon loaded blank, ready to fire twenty-one-gun salvos from each post.

A cluster of important guests crowded the bridge of the *Tennessee*—among them Secretary of the Navy William Eaton Chandler, Secretary of War Robert T. Lincoln, Congressman Edward Hurd Conger, General William Babcock Hazen, and other prominent individuals. Near the railing a tall, beautiful woman stood. She peered anxiously into the distance beyond Fort Point, toward the open sea. Everyone on the bridge strained in that same direction. The navy officers swept the horizon with their sea glasses. Suddenly smudges of smoke appeared.

"Here they come!" an officer cried.

The woman gripped the rail tensely. She turned when Secretary Chandler stepped beside her.

"He'll soon be here, Mrs. Greely," Chandler said. "Are you all right?"

Henrietta Greely flashed a smile. "Oh, yes. Yes."

"When the ships drop anchor, a longboat carrying a marine honor guard will bring your husband aboard," Chandler told her. "I'm afraid this meeting will not afford you any privacy for your reunion with Lieutenant Greely. But he no longer belongs exclusively to you. He now belongs to the nation, which is the reason for all this—" In a broad gesture he included the ships, the throngs on shore, and the notables on the bridge.

"Just now it's enough for me to know he has come safely home," Henrietta said.

A short time later four ships hove into view. Leading the incoming flotilla was the escort, the gunboat U.S.S. *Alliance*. Behind her the *Thetis*, the *Bear*, and the *Alert* sailed in line. From his place on the bridge of the *Thetis*, Dolph focused powerful binoculars on the *Tennessee*. Lowering them, he grinned at Commodore Schley.

"I saw my wife!" he exulted. "I saw Henrietta!"

He had no chance to say any more. The forts' cannon started to boom welcoming salutes. As the file of ships neared the anchored fleet, the band on the *Tennessee* could be heard playing "Home Sweet Home" across the narrowing gap of water.

Cheers rose from the sailors on the warships. Horns and whistles on shore added to the din. The rescue vessels steamed slowly past the naval craft and dropped anchor. A longboat set out from the *Tennessee*. Rowed by picked sailors from the battleship, it carried a marine detail headed by a lieutenant. The nattily dressed marines made a sharp contrast to the sailors in stark white.

The longboat warped against the *Thetis*. A gangway was lowered and the marines came aboard. A few minutes later Dolph and Commodore Schley were riding back to the *Tennessee*.

The two hundred yards that separated the *Thetis* from the battleship seemed like so many miles to Dolph. But at last he stood on the warship's deck. The marine complement came to a snappy salute. Bosuns' whistles piped him aboard. He was escorted toward the bridge.

Two Cabinet members, several Representatives and Senators, a general, and other high-ranking officers beamed down at Dolph but his eyes were fixed on Henrietta.

With a glad cry she raised her long skirt and sped down the iron stairway, ankles twinkling. Pushing past the honor guard, not paying attention to the onlooking sailors and dignitaries, she threw her arms about her husband's neck.

"Dolph! Oh, Dolph!" she sobbed, clinging to him.

On the bridge Secretary Chandler declared, "I believe we can delay the official welcome for a few minutes, gentlemen. The one which Lieutenant Greely is receiving seems far more cordial than any we might tender him."

Dolph was given a year's leave of absence upon his return. Part of the time he spent in the United States Army Hospital on Governor's Island, New York. Henrietta took up residence in New York City and visited him daily. When he had recovered sufficiently to take the trip, Dolph and Henrietta went to San Diego, where he saw his children again.

Antoinette was now six and Adola three; they moved shyly from the tall, emaciated, bearded man who stood beside their mother. For a moment Dolph kept his composure, but seeing the children strained his emotions. He turned away, with tears running down his cheeks.

Little Antoinette came to him, took his hand and looking up at him, said, "Don't be sad, Daddy, Adola and I will truly love you."

Dolph knelt and embraced the child. "This was my dream out there," he murmured.

He spent all the time he possibly could with his family. They went for drives, on picnics, and took long walks on the beach. He gained weight and strength, and no one seeing him for the first time could believe from his appearance that he had undergone such harrowing experiences.

For months after his return, lecture bureaus wanted to book Dolph on nation-wide tours at high fees. The manager of a New York theater guaranteed ten thousand dollars—a fabulous sum for those days—if Dolph would appear in a melodrama about the Lady Franklin Bay Expedition. Manufacturers sought his endorsement of their products for large sums.

He rejected all commercial use of his name. "I am neither a matinee idol nor a self-seeker. I am merely a soldier who did his duty," he stated flatly.

However, he did agree to write a book presenting the facts about the Lady Franklin Bay Expedition, to counteract the versions of it circulated in lurid books and sensational magazines.

"The American people must be told what really happened to us. For the sake of those who gave their lives, I will unfold our story without exaggeration or distortion," he announced.

His book, *The Lady Franklin Bay Expedition*, published in 1886, proved a success. Dolph revealed an unsuspected writing flair. Publishers besieged him to write more books. He continued to write, and authored works on Arctic exploration, on weather, and on flood control.

Nine of the ten nations which had participated in the Interpolar Conference decorated Dolph and the men who had come back with him. He was further honored both by the Royal Geographical Society of London and by the Paris Geographical

Society. Inexplicably only the United States awarded no medal either to Dolph or to the expedition's five other survivors. There had been six, but Corporal Joe Elison had died on the homeward voyage.

The enlisted men did receive promotions, each being presented with an extra stripe. Dolph strongly recommended Sergeant Brainard for a commission. This was acted upon favorably and Brainard returned to duty as second lieutenant. Years later, wearing the star of a brigadier general, he assumed command of the Signal Corps.

(With the exceptions of Brainard and Francis Long, who rose to sergeant and served a long time as assistant meteorologist in the United States Weather Station at New York City, nothing is known about the later activities of the other survivors.)

Dolph was promoted to captain in 1886. At the time he was serving as General Hazen's personal aide. The general's health was failing and the administration of the Signal Corps fell on Dolph. He often felt that the avalanche of paper work—the forms, reports, and requisitions—would bury him. But he worked industriously and developed into an able administrative officer.

Hazen was finally hospitalized for a lingering and fatal illness. Dolph visited his failing commander every day. With his life ebbing, Hazen dwelled upon the Lady Franklin Bay Expedition and blamed himself for the deaths that had occurred.

"I should have sailed with the *Neptune*," Hazen

insisted. "If I had been aboard, she would have made her way to your camp."

"General, that's all over now. You mustn't upset yourself. It's all ended. Besides, the relief ships simply couldn't make it. The weather stopped them. It would have stopped anyone."

"I belonged in the field with my men, Greely. If I had been with the relief expeditions, I could be certain everything possible was done. Now I shall never be sure. Perhaps a more determined effort would have saved all those lives. It is such doubt which gives me no rest," Hazen said hoarsely.

After an illness of several months' duration, fifty-seven-year-old William Babcock Hazen died on January 16, 1887. His death left the Signal Corps without a commanding officer, although Dolph still acted as administrative head.

Two weeks later, February 1, 1887, President Grover Cleveland signed an executive order appointing Dolph as chief signal officer and promoting him to brigadier general, the rank for which that office called.

As head of the Signal Corps, Dolph spent the ensuing years building and improving the organization. He set up a Signal Corps photographic section which took pictures of both military and historical interest. Always conscious of history, Dolph established the War Department Library, which contained old army journals, diaries, reports, and letters. One of his most important contributions to historians resulted from an accidental discovery when a large storage room in the old War Department building was cleaned out. Among the debris slated for the rubbish heap were a number of cardboard boxes filled with photograph negatives on glass. The plates had been made by the great cameraman Matthew Brady during the Civil War. They formed a priceless pictorial record of the war, including scenes of battlefields, behind the lines, portraits of national figures and soldiers of all ranks.

Luckily a Signal Corps officer, rummaging through the boxes piled up for the junk cart, recognized the Brady negatives. These same pictures had been the object of a long search. Shortly after the war they had been placed in that storage room and forgotten. The officer reported his find to Dolph, who had the boxes loaded on a Signal Corps wagon and hauled away to safety in the National Archives, thus saving the Brady photographs for future generations.

Through the years Dolph constantly had to battle conservatives both in Congress and in the War Department. This faction blocked Dolph's plans for modernizing the Signal Corps. In 1890 the reactionaries voted down all funds for the development of new Signal Corps equipment. Dolph promptly struck back by making a speaking tour of the country.

"I shall let the American people know that our national defense is being sabotaged by pennypinching, narrow-minded men more interested in money than in public security," he said.

Dolph was still a popular figure. The public had not forgotten the Lady Franklin Bay Expedition.

His speeches aroused the voters. They raised such a clamor that the Signal Corps was granted all the funds necessary and Dolph was able to launch a program for the improvement of military communications.

That year he introduced into general military service a telephone especially designed for operation in the field. Most European armies were already equipped with such devices. All tests demonstrated the telephone's practicability—but there was still opposition to it from old regular army men who resented any change. They even tried to convince the Secretary of War to abolish the Signal Corps. "The conveyance of military orders is not a proper object for the existence of a separate branch within the army," they argued.

Dolph squelched this senile uprising by threatening to take his case to the people again. The attempts to scuttle the Signal Corps promptly ended.

The years passed placidly and in 1898, except for occasional Indian troubles, the United States was enjoying an era of peace and prosperity. The small regular army (twenty-five thousand officers and men) carried out its normal functions of policing the border and manning the frontier forts.

Life had been settled and pleasant for Dolph in the fourteen years since his return from Lady Franklin Bay. The Greely family lived in a spacious old house on the outskirts of Washington. There were six children (four daughters—Antoinette, Adola, Rose, and Gertrude—and two sons—John and Adolphus, Jr.). It was a happy, close-knit family, and the big house echoed with laughter and song as the Greelys gathered around the piano after dinner for a group "sing" with Henrietta playing the accompaniment.

Dolph was fifty-four years old, with thirty-seven years of military service behind him. Soon he could retire, and then he would travel with Henrietta to visit the capitals of the world.

No thoughts of war marred the night of February 15, 1898. True, some tension existed with Spain over the treatment of Cuban revolutionaries seeking to free their country from Madrid's cruel domination. But no one seriously believed anything was likely to result from this friction.

In fact, the U.S.S. *Maine,* one of the newest battleships in the Atlantic fleet, had been sent to Cuba, on a good-will mission. She anchored in Havana Bay and her officers and men were graciously treated by the Spanish officials. The rift between the two countries seemed to be mending.

At midnight Dolph and Henrietta returned from a dinner party. They were preparing for bed when a horseman clattered up to the gate. Moments later, someone pounded on the door.

"Who can that be?" Dolph wondered as he slipped into his dressing gown and hurried downstairs. When he opened the door, a dust-covered Signal Corps lieutenant saluted him.

"What are you doing here, Lieutenant Gresham?" Dolph asked.

"Sir, the battleship *Maine* has been blown up in Havana harbor. Two hundred and fifty men went down with the ship. The report just came over the transoceanic cable. You are to report at the War Department immediately."

Dolph stood silently for a moment. Then he sighed softly. "Two hundred and fifty men. All the widows and children. What a pity! I'll get dressed at once, Gresham."

Henrietta appeared at the head of the stairs. "Is anything wrong, Dolph?" she called down.

He looked at her. "I'll be there in a moment, my dear," he said, slowly mounting the staircase, wondering how to tell her such ugly news.

• • • CHAPTER 17

The Curtain Falls

IN APRIL, 1898, THE UNITED STATES declared war on Spain over the sinking of the *Maine* and the question of Cuban independence. The army was poorly prepared for war, especially in the supply and transportation sections. But the Signal Corps was ready and Dolph rushed communications units to Tampa, Florida, the chief port of embarkation for troops bound for the theater of war in Cuba and Porto Rico. Dolph had prepared plans which provided for Signal Corps teams to be attached to infantry, artillery, and cavalry units to operate communications.

Signal corpsmen went ashore with the shock troops that landed on Cuba and Porto Rico. The skilled linesmen hauled portable telegraphic equipment to the very front and strung back their wires even while the infantry was digging its rifle pits.

Dolph shuttled between Tampa and Washington. He made inspection trips to the fighting fronts, both in Cuba and in Porto Rico, where he saw the field telephone being used effectively in combat for the first time by American forces.

The Curtain Falls

However, while he was kept busy running the Signal Corps, Dolph managed to carry out one of the major intelligence coups of the war. On a rainy March afternoon, even before the declaration of war, Dolph, dressed in civilian clothes, waited in a Tampa, Florida, waterfront café, pretending to be more interested in his drink than in anything else. After he had been there awhile, a man joined him. They talked in low tones for a long time. No one in that Tampa bar realized that the chief signal officer of the United States Army and a newspaperman from Santiago, Cuba (unfortunately, there is no record of the reporter's name), had arranged a clever bit of espionage.

Tampa was the terminus of the commercial cable line that ran into Santiago. The newsman, using a code which he had worked out with Dolph, sent information to the Signal Corps chief in the news stories he cabled from Santiago. All dispatches from him were promptly rushed to Dolph.

When the conflict actually broke out in April, 1898, the United States Atlantic Fleet steamed for Havana to engage the Spanish Navy in those waters. Admiral William Sampson, senior United States naval officer of the fleet, deployed his ships in accordance with the belief that the Spanish, under Admiral Pascual Cervera y Topete, were actually heading to Havana. All American strategy revolved around the disposition of the Navy—and if Cervera took his squadron anywhere but to Havana, the Americans would find themselves outmaneuvered.

One day Dolph's agent in Cuba cabled in code that Cervera, commanding a powerful fleet, was actually arriving in Santiago harbor. Dolph rushed to President William McKinley with the news that Cervera's flotilla had been located.

The President showed his astonishment. "You must be mistaken, General Greely. Admiral Sampson has positive proof that the enemy fleet is en route to Havana."

"Mr. President," Dolph said, "this message is not an hour old. It is the last word on Cervera."

McKinley pursed his lips thoughtfully. "Can you vouch for your informant?" he asked.

"Sir, I will stake my own career that this report is true."

"That's good enough, General. I shall send Sampson the necessary orders. But if this proves incorrect, I will hold you responsible," the President said firmly.

Sampson grumblingly sent a naval force to Santiago—and those ships, under Dolph's old friend Winfield Scott Schley, now a commodore, not only found Cervera's vessels at anchor in Santiago but also managed to bottle up the Spanish fleet. Finally, on July 2, 1898, the Spanish tried to break out—only to be destroyed by Schley.

Combined with an earlier American naval triumph—that of Admiral Dewey in Manila Bay, across the Pacific off the Philippines—the battle at Santiago marked the annihilation of the Spanish Navy. With its sea power smashed, Spain sued for

The Curtain Falls

peace and surrendered unconditionally on July 17, 1898.

The year 1898 was a restless one. In Alaska's Klondike region, gold had been discovered. Thousands of young Americans swarmed into that frozen country. At the war's end the United States took the Philippines (it had already purchased Hawaii) and thus extended its possessions far out into the Pacific. Closer to home, Porto Rico was ceded to the United States and for the first time the nation became a colonial power.

These acquisitions brought additional duties to Dolph and the Signal Corps. He directed the construction of an island-wide telegraph system in Porto Rico, and another in Cuba. From the tropics he moved up into Alaska. In climates that reached sixty-seven below zero the Signal Corps laid twenty-two hundred miles of telegraph line.

Dolph was not yet finished with this kind of field work. A native nationalist movement, led by one Emilio Aguinaldo, which had long fought for independence from Spain, started an insurrection to drive out the Americans. A bitter, vicious war broke out in 1900.

No one knew where Aguinaldo would strike next. His wily followers ambushed American units and fled back into the jungle. Dolph took a Signal Corps detachment to the Philippines. "The only way we can smoke out Aguinaldo is to carry communications from one army post to the other. It's the same way we fought the Indians. I intend to run telegraph and telephone wires until there's no place Aguinaldo can move without the army being informed."

The jungles were cruel and deadly—malaria took its toll—and at one time Dolph could muster only one hundred healthy men out of three hundred. But his work parties hacked their way through and the wire was strung from place to place.

Despite his rank and age, Dolph labored alongside the men. Once he helped beat off a guerilla attack. He nursed the sick, encouraged the healthy, and urged his men to greater efforts until, less than a year later, the communications network he had set out to build was an actuality. It materially aided the army to track down Aguinaldo and subdue the insurrection.

With these tasks behind him Dolph returned to the United States and again devoted himself to developments and experiments in the field of communication. He also created a new code for sending weather bulletins (the Weather Bureau was still being operated by the Signal Corps) and supervised the publication of a crop bulletin for farmers.

But, with all his activities, Dolph had never forgotten one youthful dream. Although nearly forty years had passed, he still remembered Professor Thaddeus Lowe's balloon hovering high above the battle lines at Fair Oaks.

In 1902 Professor Samuel Langley, an inventor, completed a motor-driven flying machine which he called an "aerodrome." The flimsy craft actually flew across the Potomac.

Dolph was convinced there was a place for an

The Curtain Falls

air arm in the army. As he had in 1862, he still believed that aircraft could be used offensively as well as for reconnaissance. Langley's "aerodrome" stirred the hope that this frail machine of wire, balsa wood, and canvas might be the proper aerial vehicle for the army.

He convinced Langley that it was the professor's duty to build an "aerodrome" suitable for military purposes. The professor was reluctant to accept. His health was not good and the performance of his original flying machine had disappointed him. However, he finally agreed to work on such a craft.

Dolph squeezed a seventy-five-thousand dollar appropriation from Congress to equip a workshop for Langley. The much-publicized "aerodrome" was ready for a trial in the summer of 1903. The machine, with Langley at the controls, was trundled out of its shed before an audience that included President Theodore Roosevelt. Its motor spluttered to life. The "aerodrome" rolled forward, rose a few feet, wobbled in the air, and came down with a thud. Langley stepped out of the wreckage uninjured, but the ridicule that followed his failure sent him into retirement and he died, soon after, a heartbroken, frustrated man.

A few months later, in December, Orville and Wilbur Wright launched the first powered aircraft at Kitty Hawk, North Carolina, and the world stepped into a new age. While he was disappointed by Langley's failure, Dolph was much encouraged by the Wright brothers' success.

"Someday we shall see flying machines in such

numbers that they will blot out the sun," he predicted.

He had developed keen interest in wireless telegraphy, the forerunner of radio. By the turn of the century, several wireless stations were in operation and some ships were equipped with transmitters to send messages by that medium.

In 1903 Dolph attended the First International Wireless Conference, held in Berlin. He met Guglielmo Marconi, the father of wireless telegraphy, and famous scientists from all over the world. The conference formulated the first international radio regulations and established standard procedures for the use of wireless telegraphy at sea. It was there that the present-day SOS signal—three dots, three dashes, three dots—was accepted as the universal signal for ships in distress.

After thirty years of unbroken service in the Signal Corps, Dolph left the branch he had done so much to develop—the date was February 10, 1906. He was raised to major general and assigned as commandant of the Pacific Division, United States Army, with headquarters in the Presidio, San Francisco. Dolph's successor as chief signal officer was Brigadier General David L. Brainard, the faithful sergeant of Lady Franklin Bay and Eskimo Point.

San Francisco was rocked by violent earthquakes on April 18, 1906. Disastrous fires followed the tremors. For the seventh time in its history, the city of two hundred thousand people was devastated. Hundreds of buildings were destroyed, tens of

The Curtain Falls

thousands made homeless. The property damages were incalculable; the loss of life was high.

The morning the earthquake struck, Dolph was on a train heading for Washington, where he was to attend the wedding of his daughter, Rose. He received the news in Chicago and promptly returned to San Francisco. By the time he arrived, his second in command, General Leonard Funston, a Spanish–American War hero, had placed the stricken city under martial law. Patrols of soldiers with fixed bayonets on loaded rifles patrolled the rubble-strewn streets. The fires, however, still raged unchecked.

Dolph stared horrified at the devastation. Block after block of the great metropolis lay in ruins. Wherever he turned, there was wreckage and destruction. He walked for miles through the ravaged city and saw the dead lying on the sidewalk, while the injured lay groaning helplessly.

Dolph went to his shattered headquarters in the Presidio. Through the broken windows he could see smoke billowing up from the fires. Turning to a map of the city, he checked off the area still endangered by the conflagration.

"General Funston," he ordered, "you will send engineers to dynamite all buildings in the path of the flames."

"That means we'll have to demolish half of San Francisco," Funston noted wryly.

"If the whole city has to be blown off the map, we will stop those fires," Dolph snapped.

The demolitions continued for two days, but finally halted the fires. With the fires out, Dolph turned to helping the injured, sheltering the homeless, and feeding the hungry. Dazed earthquake refugees wandered aimlessly about the shattered streets.

Under Dolph's orders, soldiers herded them into huge tent cantonments which the army had set up. Soup kitchens were put into operation. Tons of rations, clothing, and medical supplies poured into San Francisco. The troops were reinforced by units of the California National Guard and additional companies of regulars. Every doctor and nurse in San Francisco and its environs was mobilized under the supervision of army surgeons. Typhoid and smallpox epidemics loomed as a potential danger.

"I want every man, woman, and child in San Francisco vaccinated against smallpox. No one is to take a mouthful of drinking water that has not been boiled," Dolph commanded. "Anyone caught looting is to be shot at once," he added.

These stringent measures prevented epidemics—and after several looters were shot, pillaging ceased. In an amazingly short period San Francisco recovered from the calamity. Its grateful citizens presented Dolph with a scroll signed by thousands of residents.

After this episode his army career soon ended. He retired in 1907 and took up permanent residence in Washington, where he kept busy attending radio and wireless conferences and writing.

In 1911 his beloved Henrietta died. He accepted

The Curtain Falls

her death stoically and, although grieving for her, he did not give up his work.

When the United States entered the first World War in 1917, Dolph returned to temporary duty as a special adviser to the Signal Corps. That was his last military endeavor.

He had lived to see airplanes carrying warfare into the sky. After the war another of his predictions became a reality—as he had foreseen in 1862, passengers traveled by air in giant planes.

He lived on, loved and respected by all. On his ninety-first birthday, March 27, 1935, President Franklin Roosevelt presented him with the Congressional Medal of Honor in belated appreciation of his achievements.

The day was a trying one for the old soldier. His ninety-first birthday was celebrated at a party to which hundreds of guests had been invited. Presents were showered upon him and thousands of telegrams bringing birthday greetings from all over the world were delivered to him.

That evening, after the festivities were over, he sat alone in his bedroom. He held the Congressional Medal of Honor in his hand and thought about the events that had brought this coveted award to him. He remembered dimly the faces of the men with whom he had worked—the men of Lady Franklin Bay, the youths who had marched off to the Civil War with him. . . . He remembered all that had gone to make up his life and he smiled at the memories—it was good to dream of all his friends.

On October 20, 1935, at 9:00 P.M. Dolph died in Walter Reed Hospital after a brief illness. Still another of his predictions had come true.

He would not see another springtime.

Chronology

1844: March 25. Adolphus Washington Greely born, Newburyport, Massachusetts.

1861: April 2. Fort Sumter bombarded, signalling outbreak of Civil War.
Dolph Greely enlists in Newburyport Rifles.
May 25. Newburyport Rifles mustered into Federal service as Company D, 19th Massachusetts U.S. Volunteers.
October 21. Battle of Ball's Bluff, Virginia. Greely under fire for first time.

1862: September 17. Wounded at Battle of Antietam.
December 13. Battle of Fredericksburg, Virginia.

1863: January. Commissioned 2nd Lieutenant, U.S. Volunteers. Assigned to 81st Regiment, U.S. Volunteers (Colored).

1865: April 9. Lee surrenders at Appomattox. Civil War virtually over. Greely decides to remain in army. At war's end he is Brevet-Major.

May. Greely accepted in Regular Army, with rank of 2nd Lieutenant. Assigned to 36th U.S. Infantry, Fort Sanders, Wyoming.

1865– Serves with 36th Infantry on frontier, fight-
1868: ing Indians, guarding stage and mail routes.

1868: May 12. Greely transfers to Signal Corps.

July 20. Reports to General Albert James Myer, Fortress Monroe, Virginia, and is placed in charge of Weather Bureau, then under Signal Corps.

1868– Does exceptional job in building Weather
1873: Bureau, is responsible for important innovations in its operation. Earns reputation as "Father of Weather Bureau."

1873: September. Greely assigned by General Myer to build telegraph line in Wyoming.

1876: After three years in field setting up telegraph networks, is sent to Europe to observe Signal Corps in British, French and Austrian armies. Returns in September.

December 24. Completes telegraph line from Sante Fe, New Mexico, to San Diego, California. Meets Henrietta Nesmith.

1877: Marries Henrietta Nesmith.

Chronology

1881: Assigned to lead Lady Franklin Bay Expedition.
August. Arrives at Lady Franklin Bay.

1881–
1884: Greely Expedition makes first scientific surveys and studies in Northern Greenland. Relief ships fail to arrive.

1883: August 9. Greely starts retreat to Cape Sabine.
September 29. Arrives at Eskimo Point, twenty miles north of Cape Sabine. Exhausted men can go no further. Party encamps to await rescue.

1884: June 22. Relief expedition under Captain Winfield Schott Schley finds Greely. Only six, including Greely, survive ordeal.
August 8. Greely Expedition survivors arrive in United States.

1887: Greely, promoted to Brigadier General, appointed head of Signal Corps.

1898: U.S. declares war on Spain. Under Greely's leadership Signal Corps plays decisive role.

1900–
1903: Signal Corps strings thousands of miles of telephone and telegraph wires in Cuba, Porto Rico, Alaska and Philippines under Greely's supervision.

Chronology

1903: Attends First International Wireless Conference in Berlin, meets Marconi.

1906: Leaves Signal Corps on promotion to Major General. Assumes command of Pacific Division, U.S. Army, with headquarters in San Francisco.
April 18. San Francisco Earthquake. Greely in charge of relief for stricken city.

1907: Retires from army, devotes himself to research in wireless radio, radio telegraphy and wireless communications.

1911: Henrietta Nesmith Greely dies.

1917: Greely called to temporary duty with Signal Corps as special advisor in World War I.

1935: March 27. Decorated with Congressional Medal of Honor by President Franklin D. Roosevelt.
October 20. Greely dies in Walter Reed Hospital at age of 91.

Personnel of the Lady Franklin Bay Expedition August, 1881-August, 1884

1st Lieutenant Adolphus W. Greely, 5th Cavalry*

2nd Lieutenant Frederick F. Kislingbury, 11th Infantry

2nd Lieutenant James B. Lockwood, 23rd Infantry

Sergeant Edward Israel, Signal Corps

Sergeant Winfield S. Jewell, Signal Corps

Sergeant George Rice, Signal Corps

Sergeant Hampden Gardiner, Signal Corps

Sergeant William H. Cross, General Service

Sergeant David Ralston, Signal Corps

Sergeant David L. Brainard, 2nd Cavalry*

---

* Indicates a survivor.

Personnel of the Expedition

Sergeant David Linn, 2nd Cavalry

Corporal Nicholas Salor, 2nd Cavalry

Corporal Joseph Elison, 10th Infantry**

Private Roderick R. Schneider, 1st Artillery

Private Charles Henry, 5th Cavalry

Private Maurice Connell, 3rd Cavalry*

Private Jacob Bender, 9th Infantry

Private Francis Long, 9th Infantry*

Private Henry Biederbeck, 17th Infantry*

Private Julius Frederick, 2nd Cavalry*

Private William Ellison, 2nd Cavalry

Octave Pavy, M.D.—Surgeon, U.S. Army

Jens Edwards—Eskimo Hunter

Frederick Thorley Christiansen—Eskimo Hunter

** Elison died on the way back after rescue.

Suggestions for Further Reading

BOOKS

Adams, John G. B. *Reminiscences of the 19th Massachusetts Regiment.* Boston: Wright & Potter, 1899.
Brainard, David L. *The Outpost of the Lost.* Indianapolis: The Bobbs-Merrill Company, 1929.
Greely, Adolphus W. *Earthquakes in California.* Washington, D.C.: Government Printing Office, 1906.
——. *Explorers and Travelers.* New York: Charles Scribner's Sons, 1904.
——. *Handbook of Alaska.* New York: Charles Scribner's Sons, 1925.
——. *Handbook of Polar Discoveries.* Boston: Little, Brown and Company, 1906.
——. *Three Years of Arctic Service.* New York: Charles Scribner's Sons, 1886.
——. *True Tales of Arctic Heroism.* New York: Charles Scribner's Sons, 1912.
Mitchell, William. *General Greely: The Story of a*

Suggestions for Further Reading

Great American. New York: G. P. Putnam's Sons, 1936.

Patch, Joseph D. *The Battle of Ball's Bluff*. Leesburg, Virginia: Potomac Press, 1958.

Schley, W. S. *The Rescue of Greely*. New York: Charles Scribner's Sons, 1885.

PERIODICALS

Harper's Weekly, August 1884.
Leslie's Weekly, August 1884.
London Illustrated News, August 1884.

NEWSPAPERS

The following newspapers of August 4–24, 1884:

New York *Herald*
New York *Times*
New York *Tribune*
New York *World*
Washington *Star*

Index

abolitionists, 8, 64
"Adeste Fideles," 111
Aguinaldo, Emilio, 155
airplanes, 3, 156-57, 161. See also balloons
Alabama, 52
Alaska, 90, 155
Alert, 137, 139, 142
Alliance, U.S.S., 142
Anderson, Major Robert ("Bob"), 8
Antarctic, 90
Antietam Creek, Md., battle, 51
Arctic, 3, 90-91, 92, 93. See also Lady Franklin Bay Expedition
Army, U.S., 1, 137
Army of Northern Virginia (Confederate), 42, 51
Army of the Potomac (Union), 41-45, 51-52, 58, 117
Arthur, President Chester Alan, 4, 136-37
Atlantic Coast, 74
Atlantic fleet, 141-43, 153
"Auld Lang Syne," 26

Austria, 90
Austrian Signal Corps, 87
automobiles, 3

Bad Lands, 79
Baffin Bay, 93, 100
Baker, Colonel, 31
balloons, for reconnaissance, 44-46, 156. See also airplanes
Ball's Bluff, Va., battle, 29-39, 49, 60, 71
Baltimore, 20
Bannock Indians, 65, 66, 67
"Battle Hymn of the Republic, The," 6, 42
Bay Staters, 4, 7. See also Massachusetts
Bear, 137, 138, 142
Beauregard, General, 8
Belle Island, prison, 59
Bender, Pvt. Jacob, 126, 127, 129
Berlin, 158
Biederbeck, Pvt. Henry, cook, 102, 134-35
Bigelow, Col. William, 66, 67-68

Index

Bismarck, N.D., 90
"Bloody Lane," 51
Boston, 11, 20, 23
Brady, Matthew, 148
Brainard, Sgt. David L., 94, 102, 105-106, 107, 112, 113, 125, 126, 127-28, 129, 130, 131, 133, 134, 135; journal, quoted, 101-102, 117; promotions, 146, 158
breastworks. *See* trenches
Brierly, Sergeant Willie, 17-18, 19, 23, 33, 59
British Signal Corps, 87
Buchanan, James, 4
Bull Run, 27
Burnside, Gen. Ambrose, 58

Caesar, Julius, 50
California, 87, 89
California National Guard, 160
Cape Hawks, 97, 116
Cape Isabella, 97, 116
Cape Sabine, 97, 98, 116, 118, 123-24, 125, 126, 127, 138
Casey, Seth, 48-50, 67
cavalry, for scouting, 44-45, 46-47
Cervera y Topete, Adm. Pascual, 153
Chandler, William Eaton, Secretary of the Navy, 137, 141-42, 144
Cheyenne Indians, 67
Chicago, 136, 159
Christiansen, Frederick Thorley, hunter, 100, 107, 117, 126, 132-33

circumpolar expeditions, U.S., 90-91
Civil War, 3, 4, 8ff., 137, 148; end of, 63-64. *See also* battles by name, etc.
Cleveland, President Grover, 4, 147
Coast Guard, 74, 75
Cobb, "Grandpa," 11, 12
Coffin, Capt. G. W., 137
Colorado, 64-65
Comanches, 82
communication, Civil War methods, 44-50. *See also* telegraph system, telephone, Signal Corps, etc.
Company D, Nineteenth Massachusetts Volunteers, 4, 24, 25, 26-37, 45
Confederates, 29, 30, 36, 44, 48, 58-59; invade North, 50-51. *See also* Rebels, battles by name, etc.
Conger, Congressman Edward Hurd, 102, 142
Congress, U.S., 2, 63, 76, 90, 136, 157
Connel, Pvt. Maurice, 110, 112, 134, 135
Coolidge, Calvin, 4
Crawford, Major Walter, 22, 23-24
Cross, Sgt. William H., 121, 122
Cross of St. George, British, 1
Cuba, 150, 152, 153, 154

Dakota Territory, 79, 82, 90
Darnestown, Md., 28, 40
Denmark, 90, 100

Index

Denver, 65
Dewey, Admiral, 154
Disko, island, 100

Edwards, Jens, hunter, 100, 105-106, 107, 109, 117, 120, 126, 132-33
Eighty-first Colored U.S. Infantry, 63-64
Eleventh Infantry, 94
Elison, Corp. Joe, 113, 126, 127, 134, 135, 146
Emancipation Proclamation, 63
Emory, Lt. William, 137, 138
Engineers, Corps of Army, 78
England, 90
Eskimo Point encampment, 124-29, 130-35, 138
Eskimo settlements, 100, 101
Etah, 101, 133
Europe, 86, 88

Fair Oaks, Va., battle, 42, 156
Far North, 92, 104-105
Fifth Cavalry, 68, 108
Fifth United States Infantry, 23
Fillmore, Millard, 4
Finland, 90
First International Wireless Conference, in Berlin, 158
Fischer, Colonel Geoffrey, 29, 31, 40, 59, 60, 61-62, 132
flood prevention, 76
Florida, 152, 153
Fort Bridger, Wyo., 67

Fort Conger (Arctic post), 102, 105, 108-14, 115-21, 124, 125
Fort Constitution, 141
Fort Point, 141, 142
Fort Sanders, Wyo., 64-65, 66-68, 77
Fort Sumter, 8, 10
Fortress Monroe, Va., 68-70, 71-77, 95
Fredericks, Pvt. Julius, cook, 102, 108, 131, 134-35
Fredericksburg, Va., battle, 58
French Signal Corps, 87
Fulton, Robert, 46
Funston, Gen. Leonard, 159

Gaines' Mill, Va., battle, 42
Galveston, Tex., 84
Garfield, President James, 4, 92, 137
Garnett, Dave, 8-13, 14-16, 19, 22, 27, 29-30, 32, 36, 37, 40, 59
Germany, 90
Glendale, Va., battle, 42
"God Rest Ye Merry Gentlemen," 111
Godhavn, an Eskimo settlement, 100
gold, discovery of, 155
"Gopher Regiment," 41
Governor's Island, N.Y., U.S. Army Hospital, 144
Grant, Ulysses, 4, 77, 84-85
Grant Land, 119
Greely, Adola (daughter), 91, 134, 136, 140, 144, 149
Greely, Adolphus, Jr. (son), 149

173

Index

Greely, Adolphus Washington ("Dolph"), appearance, 1, 12; medals, 1-2; Congressional Medal of Honor, 2-3, 5, 161; life and accomplishments recalled, 2-5, 161-62; farmer, 7-13, 19; in Rifles, 14-22; in federal service, 24-25; encampments, 26-29, 40-41, 56-62; at Ball's Bluff, 29-39; training at Darnestown, 40-41; promoted to corporal, 41; learns telegraphy 48; wounded, 51; hospitalized, 51-55; furloughed for mother's funeral, 54; sells the farm, 57-58; commissioned second lieutenant, 61-62; decides to stay in army, 63-64; at Fort Sanders, 66-69; assigned to Signal Corps, 68; chief of Weather Bureau, 69-70, 71-77; builds telegraph system in Wyoming and Dakota Territory, 77, 78-79; strings telegraph network along Texas–Mexican border, 80-85; in Europe to observe Signal Corps, 87; strings further telegraph lines, 88, 89, 90; his courtship and marriage, 89-90; first lieutenant, 91; leader of Lady Franklin Bay Expedition 91-98, 99-107, 108-14, 115-21, 122-29, 130-35; rescued, 138-40; homecoming, 141-44; writes books 145; captain, 146; chief signal officer and brigadier general, 147, 153; major general, 158; retires, 160; dies, 162. *See also* Signal Corps, Lady Franklin Bay Expedition, etc.

Greely, Antoinette (daughter), 91, 134, 136, 140, 144, 149

Greely, Frances Cobb (mother), 10-13, 19, 21-22; fatal accident, 54-55, 56-57

Greely, Gertrude (daughter), 149

Greely, Henrietta Nesmith (wife), 89-90, 91, 92-93, 111, 134, 136, 140, 142-44, 150, 151, 160

Greely, John (father), 8-9, 11, 12

Greely, John (son), 149

Greely, Rose (daughter), 149, 159

Greenland, 90, 100, 111, 121, 133, 134. *See also* Lady Franklin Bay Expedition

Gresham, Lieutenant, 150-51

Grinnell Land, 90, 93, 97, 98, 105-107, 111, 116, 118

guerilla warfare, 41, 156

Hamburg Convention, 90, 91. *See also* Interpolar Conference

Hampton Roads, Va., 44

Harding, Warren, 4

Harris, First Sergeant Waldo, 23, 29, 30, 33, 34, 35, 37, 38, 40, 52, 59

Index

Harrisburg, Pa., U.S. Military Hospital, 51-55
Harrison, Benjamin, 4
Havana, 150-51, 153
Hawaii, 155
Hayes, Rutherford B., 4, 89
Hazen, Gen. William Babcock, 91-95, 107, 142, 146-47
Hazen Lake, 106-107, 119
Henry, Pvt. Charles, 108-109, 130-32
Holland, 90
"Home Sweet Home," 110, 143
Hoover, Herbert, 4
Hudson Bay, 94

Indian fighting, 41, 65, 66-67, 69, 80, 82, 90
Interpolar Conference, 145. See also Hamburg Convention
Intrepid (balloon), 44-45
Israel, Sgt. Edward, 94, 102, 105, 106, 107, 110

"John Brown's Body," 42
Johnson, Andrew, 4
Johnston, Gen. Joe, 42

Kislingbury, 2nd Lt. Frederick F., 94, 96, 97-98 99-100, 102-103, 105, 108 110, 111-12, 115, 116, 118, 120, 122, 128, 130, 132, 134
Kittrey's Island, 141
Kitty Hawk, N.C., 157
Klondike, 155

Krebs, Fred, 12, 19, 21, 57-58

Lady Greely, steam launch, 102, 118, 119, 121, 123
Lady Franklin Bay Expedition, 3, 90; purpose of, 91; Greely chosen to lead, 92; personnel of, 92, 93-94; advance party leaves, 96; *Proteus* sails, 96; relief ships promised, 97; destination reached, 100-101; weather observations, 104-105; explorations, 105-107, 111-14, 119; Christmas (1881) celebration, 109-11; relief ships fail to arrive, 115-16, 119-21, 122-23, 135-36; achievements, 121; retreat from Fort Conger, 119-21, 122-24; supplies left by *Neptune*, 126-27; encamped at Eskimo Point, 124-29, 130-35, 138-39; on reduced rations, 128, 133-34, 135; rescue mission, 135-40. See also personnel by name
Lady Franklin Bay Expedition, The, by Greely, 145
Langley, Professor Samuel, 156-57
Lee, Robert E., 42, 50-51, 58
Leesburg, Va., 29
Legion d'Honneur, French, 1
Libby Prison, 59
Lincoln, Abraham, 4, 8, 9, 11, 47, 49, 58

Index

Lincoln, Robert T., Secretary of War, 136, 142
Lockwood, 2nd Lt. James B., 94, 105, 106, 109, 111-14, 115, 118, 119, 120, 126-27, 130, 131, 134
London, 88, 146
Long, Pvt. Francis, 72ff., 94, 112, 113, 117, 125, 126, 132, 133, 134, 135; sergeant, 146
"Lorena," 110
Louisiana, 64
Lowe, Professor Thaddeus, 44-45, 156

McCall, Captain Asa, 9, 16-19, 22, 23, 28, 29, 31, 33, 59
McClellan, Gen. George Brinton, 41-42, 44, 45, 49, 51, 53, 58
McKinley, President William, 4, 154
Madrid, 150
Maine, U.S.S., 150-51, 152
Malvern Hill, Va., battle, 43
Manassas, Va., battle in, 27-28
Manila Bay, 154
Marconi, Guglielmo, 158
Marker, Major David, 52-55
Markham, Major Quintus, 41
Maryland, 28-29, 38, 40, 50-51
Massachusetts, 4, 54
Medaglia d'Oro, Italian, 1
Merrimac, 44
Mexican border. *See* Texas
Mexican War, 12, 57
Milroy, Sgt. Fred, 79, 81-84

Mississippi, 64
Mississippi Valley, 76
Monitor, 44
Morse Code, 48
Myer, Gen. Albert James, 67, 69-70, 72, 75-77, 79, 80, 84, 85, 87-91

National Archives, 147-48
Navy, U.S., 137-40, 141-43
Negro regiments, 63-64
Neptune, 126, 127, 135, 146-47
Nesmith, Henrietta, 89-90. *See also* Greely, Henrietta Nesmith
New England, 44, 57. *See also* Newburyport
New Hampshire, 11, 141
New Mexico, 87, 89
New Orleans, La., 64
New York, 20, 86, 136, 144, 145, 146
Newburyport, Mass., 4, 7, 8, 11, 14-25, 54, 56-57, 58
Newburyport National Bank, 16, 58
Newburyport Rifles, 9, 15-19, 20-23
Newfoundland, 93, 96, 99, 137
Nineteenth Massachusetts Volunteers, 4, 24, 25, 26-37, 40-52, 59. *See also* Company D
Ninth Infantry, 94
North, 20, 42; Confederates invade, 50-51
North Carolina, 157
North Dakota, 90

176

Index

North Pole, 101, 104, 111, 114
Norway, 90

"O Little Town of Bethlehem," 111
Old Ironsides, 12
Order of St. Catherine, Russian, 1
Oregon, 90, 94
Overland Mail route, 67

Paris, 88
Paris Geographical Society, 146
Pavy, Dr. Octave, 94, 115, 126, 128
Pennsylvania, 51
Petersburg, Va., battle, 43
Petersen, Sven, 33, 34, 37, 40, 46, 52, 59
Philadelphia, 20
Philippine Islands, 3, 154, 155-56
Pierce, Franklin, 4
Point Barrow, Alaska, 90
Polk, James, 3
Port Hudson, La., 64
Porto Rico, 3, 152, 153, 155
Portsmouth, N.H., 141-44
Potomac River, 6, 28-39, 156
prefabricated shelter, first known, 95
Presidents, U.S. (1844-1935), 3-4
production of war material, 20
progress, wartime, 43-50
Proteus, 93, 94, 96, 99-104, 110, 135-36
Puerto Rico. *See* Porto Rico

railroads, 3, 43, 64
Rappahannock River, 56, 58, 60
Rebels, 9, 12, 14, 28, 32, 34, 36, 38, 41, 44, 59, 82. *See also* Southerners, Secessionists, Confederates
Revolution, American, 50
Rice, Pvt. George, 72ff.; sergeant, 94
Richmond, Va., 42, 44
Rio Grande, 80
Robeson Channel, 90, 111
Roosevelt, President Franklin Delano, 1-6, 161
Roosevelt, President Theodore, 4, 157
Royal Geographical Society of London, 145-46
runaway slaves, 11
Russia, 90

St. John's, Newf., 93, 96, 137
Salt Lake City, Utah, 67
Sampson, Adm. William, 153, 154
San Diego, 87, 89-90, 136, 144
San Francisco earthquake, 3, 158-60
Santa Fe, N.M., 87, 89
Santiago, Cuba, 153, 154
Schley, Capt. Winfield Scott, 137, 138-40, 143; commodore, 154
Seavey's Island, 141
Secessionists, 9, 14, 20
Second Cavalry, 94
Secretary of War, 17
Sharpsburg, Md. (Battle of Antietam), 51

Index

Signal Corps, U.S., 1, 2, 3, 67-70, 74, 76, 77, 78, 79, 87, 88, 91-92, 94, 146-51 152-61

Signal Service, U.S., 47-50, 67

"Silent Night, Holy Night," 111

Sioux Indians, 67

Sixth Massachusetts Regiment, 20

slavery, 9, 11, 63-64

Smith Sound, 97, 116, 118, 119, 122-23, 125, 127, 132, 134, 136, 138

SOS signal, 158

South Carolina, 14

Southerners, 8-9, 20, 38. *See also* Rebels, Secessionists

Spain, 150, 152, 154-55. *See also* Spanish–American War

Spanish–American War, 3, 150-51, 152-55, 159

Stanton, Edwin, Secretary of War, 47

Stars and Stripes, in Arctic, 102, 121

Stone, Gen. Charles E., 28, 35-37

Sweden, 90

Taft, William, 4

Tampa, Fla., 152, 153

Taylor, Lt. Col. Thaddeus, 40-41

Taylor, Zachary, 4

telegraph system, in Philippines, and Porto Rico, 3, 152, 155-56; in Civil War, 44-50; for weather reports, 74, 75, 76, 156; linking forts in Wyoming and Dakota Territory, 77, 78-79; along Texas–Mexican border, 80-85; Santa Fe–San Diego, 87-88, 89; Bismarck, N.D.–Oregon, 90; in Cuba and Alaska, 152, 155. *See also* wireless telegraphy

Telegraphic Bureau, U.S., 47-48

telephone, field, 3, 149, 152, 155-56

Tennessee, U.S.S., 141. 143

"Tenting Tonight," 110

Texas, 80-85

Thetis, 137, 138, 140, 142-43

Thirty-sixth Infantry Regiment, 63, 64-68

Tilden, Samuel, 89

Townsend, Mayor Lawrence, 14, 54, 57

trenches, use of, 41

Twenty-third Infantry, 94

Tyler, John, 3

underground railway, 11

Union, 20, 43. *See also* battles by name, etc.

Union troops, 58-59; at Ball's Bluff, 29-39

United States, 90, 92, 135-37

United States Ford, 50

United States Range, 107, 119

Vicksburg, Miss., 64

Vienna, 88

Index

Virginia, 27, 29-39, 41-44, 56, 84, 85, 89. *See also* Fortress Monroe

Walter Reed Hospital, 162
War Department, 45, 47, 62, 68, 148, 151
War Department Library, 147-48
War of 1812, 12, 50
Washington, D.C., 1-6, 20, 26, 61, 62, 75, 79, 80, 84-85, 88, 89, 90, 91, 96, 119, 136, 149-51, 152, 159, 160
Weather Bureau, U.S., 69-70, 71-79, 94, 156
Weather Station, U.S., at N.Y.C., 146
Whisler, Pvt., 112
White House, 1-6, 84-85
White Oak Swamp, Va., 84
Whitlock, Elihu, 56
Williamsburg, Va., battle, 43
Wilson, Woodrow, 4
wireless telegraphy, 158
Woodson, Pvt. Ben, 72ff.
World War, first, 161
Wright brothers, 157
Wyoming, 64-65, 66-69, 77, 78-79, 82

Yantic, 135
Yorktown, Va., battle, 43

POCKET BOOKS

ARCHWAY
PAPERBACKS

Other titles you will enjoy

29506 CAVE OF DANGER, by Bryce Walton. When Matt discovers a big, new cave, he and his friend make the risky descent underground and plunge straight into terrifying adventure. (75¢)

29542 HILLS END, by Ivan Southall. Illustrated by Jim Phillips. Cut off from all adult help, surrounded by wild mountains and a flooded river, seven boys and girls fight for survival on their own. (75¢)

29569 THE BLACK STONE KNIFE, by Alice Marriott. Illustrated by Harvey Weiss. Wolf Boy, a Kiowa Indian, takes an adventurous journey through a strange, new land. He meets his first white man, makes a daring escape from Apaches, and has a deadly battle with a water monster. (75¢)

29504 CHILDREN OF THE RESISTANCE, by Lore Cowan. Eight dramatic true stories of teen-agers who fought for freedom in the underground resistance movement in Europe during World War II. (75¢)

(If your bookseller does not have the titles you want, you may order them by sending the retail price, plus 25¢ for postage and handling to: Mail Service Department, POCKET BOOKS, a division of Simon & Schuster, Inc., 1 West 39th Street, New York, N. Y. 10018. Please enclose check or money order—do not send cash.)